THE WI BOOK OF
POULTRY
AND GAME

PAT HESKETH

EBURY
PRESS

ACKNOWLEDGEMENTS

Illustrated by Cooper-West Graphic Design
Edited by Sue Parish and Bridget Daly
Designed by Clare Clements
Cover photography by James Jackson

The author, Pat Hesketh, is the WI's
Home Economics and Specialised Crafts
Adviser; she travels extensively lecturing
and tutoring WI members in all aspects of
home economics and crafts.

Published by Ebury Press,
National Magazine House,
72, Broadwick Street,
London W1V 2BP

ISBN 0 85223 438 4

First impression 1985

© Copyright WI Books Limited

Filmset by
D.P. Media Limited, Hitchin, Hertfordshire

Reproduced, printed and bound in Great Britain by
Hazell Watson & Viney Limited,
Member of the BPCC Group,
Aylesbury, Bucks.

CONTENTS

INTRODUCTION

Poultry and game have been of great interest to the breeder, sportsman, hunter and cook for many hundreds of years.

Country people have always kept domestic poultry, particularly chickens and often geese and ducks. Rabbits and hares were regularly made into tasty dishes, though they would be considered luxury food by some poor families. Quite often they may have been poached from the local landowner's fields. The more exotic game such as pheasant, partridge and venison regularly graced the tables of the gentry.

Nowadays, poultry is readily available and specialist shops display a good range of game birds and animals which can provide something different for a dinner party or that special celebration meal.

This book deals with the choice and preparation of poultry and game – both feather and fur. It gives many interesting and exciting, as well as traditional, ways of cooking and serving.

Choosing poultry and game
Chicken. There are various types available.

Poussin: 6–10 weeks old; 700 g (1½ lb). Usually split down the backbone and best roasted, spit-roasted or grilled. One bird will serve 2 people.

Broiler: Spring chicken; 3 months old; 900 g–1.2 kg (2–2½ lb). May be roasted, pot-roasted or sautéed. One bird will serve 3–4 people.

Roaster: 6 months old; 1.5–1.8 kg (3–4 lb); the most popular size. Usually roasted or pot-roasted. One bird will serve 4–6.

Large roaster: 9 months old; up to 3.6 kg (8 lb). Cockerel which has been specially fattened for the table. Can be roasted; is a good size for boning out. One bird will serve up to 10 people.

Boiler: 12–18 months old; 1.8–2.5 kg (4–6 lb). Good for making broths, especially cock-a-leekie (see page 26) and for cold dishes served with sauces. There is a tendency for them to become fatty, so gentle boiling is required, then cooling, thus enabling the fat to be skimmed off.

Turkey. A hen turkey has a small frame and more meat in ratio to bone than a stag (male turkey), though the latter is often preferred for flavour. Whole turkeys are available as follows:

Clean-plucked:	Head, legs and intestines intact. Should be dressed as for chicken (see page 8).
Oven-ready:	Giblets packed separately; ready for the oven.
Frozen:	Giblets not usually included. Frozen turkey should be defrosted slowly in a cool place (not in the fridge) for 36–48 hours.

Turkey is also available (fresh and frozen) as turkey leg joints, turkey leg roasts and turkey breast roasts.

A 4.5–6.0-kg (10–13-lb) bird will serve 10–12 people, or 8 people with enough left over for a cold dish. A 4-kg (9-lb) frozen turkey is equivalent to a 5.4-kg (12-lb) clean-plucked turkey.

A 7.2–9.0-kg (16–20-lb) turkey should provide several meals for a family party of 6–8 people.

A 9.0–11.5-kg (20–25-lb) bird or larger will be required for a large household, and when lots of cold turkey is needed. When purchasing an extra-large turkey, your oven measurements should be checked beforehand.

Duck. Young ducks up to 8 months old may be roasted or spit-roasted. Birds over 12 months should be casseroled. They are at their best in early summer. They have a shallow breast and feed fewer people than a chicken of corresponding weight. A 1.8-kg (4-lb) bird will serve 3–4 people.

Goose. Available throughout the year but at its best at Christmas-time. A mature goose will weigh 4.5–6.3 kg (10–14 lb) and, like duck, is wasteful. Allow 450–550 g (1–1¼ lb) per person – a 4.5-kg (10-lb) bird will serve 8 people.

Guinea-fowl. A tasty bird with a flavour between chicken and pheasant. A young guinea-fowl is tender and good roasted. Older birds should be casseroled. Any recipe for chicken and pheasant may be used. One bird will serve 4–5 people.

Pheasants. They are sold by the brace – a cock and a hen. A young cock will have short, rounded spurs which become longer and pointed with age. A young hen has soft pliable feet which harden with age. Young birds have pointed feathers – rounded feathers indicate age. Young birds are excellent roasted, but older birds should be pot-roasted or casseroled. One pheasant will serve 2–4, depending on its size.

Partridge. There are two varieties – the English, or grey, partridge, which is considered to be better-flavoured than the larger French, or red-legged, partridge. The latter, although of continental origin, tends to be more common. A young bird will have a soft beak and pointed feathers. Young birds are excellent plain-roasted. One bird serves 1–2 people.

Grouse. Young birds have bright eyes, soft pliable feet and smooth legs and a soft pliable tip to the breastbone. In older birds the bones become hard and the feet scaly with sharp claws. Young birds are good oven- or spit-roasted; older birds require moist cooking by casseroling or can be used in pies and terrines. One plump bird serves 2 people.

Black game or black grouse. A member of the grouse family and about twice the size of a grouse. With the exception of very young birds, the meat is rather dry and a moist cooking method is recommended. Any recipes suitable for grouse may be used, but longer cooking time must be allowed. One bird serves 3–4.

Ptarmigan or white grouse. The smallest grouse, ptarmigan has not such a good flavour as grouse but young birds have a delicate taste when roasted. Older birds may be bitter and should be casseroled, with well-flavoured ingredients. Any recipe for grouse may be used. One bird serves 1–2 people.

Capercaillie. The largest member of the grouse family. Young birds have supple feet and smooth pliable legs, they may be roasted. Older birds have rough scaly legs and should be casseroled. The gizzard has an unpleasant taste and should not be used for giblet stock. A cock bird will serve 6–8 people; a hen bird will serve 3–4 people.

Wild duck. A collective name for a wide variety of duck species; the most usual ones being mallard, wigeon and teal. Although the mallard is the largest and the best known, it is the little teal which has most flavour. Unlike the domestic duck, the flesh is dry and needs plenty of fat for roasting. A mallard should serve 2–3 people, but teal will serve only one person. A duck shot on the fore-shore may have a 'fishy' flavour. This can be overcome by placing an onion or potato inside the cavity, and poaching the bird in salted water for 20 minutes. Rinse and dry thoroughly before roasting in the usual way.

Woodcock. Difficult to obtain in the shops and considered by many to be the best-flavoured of all game birds. Once a breakfast delicacy, it is now served for dinner either as a starter or main course. A minimum of one bird per person should be allowed

Snipe. A small bird and a great delicacy. One bird per person will do for a starter, but two for a main course.

Quail. Rare in the wild but now reared on game farms, this little bird is now widely available from poulterers and delicatessens and can also be bought frozen. One bird per person is needed for a starter and two for a main course.

Pigeon. All pigeons can be eaten but it is the wood-pigeon which can have a gamey flavour. It is readily available, cheap and nutritious. Young birds can be roasted, but for best results, long, slow cooking is advisable. For a pie, they are best pre-cooked.

Rabbit. Rabbits are at their best between 3 and 4 months old. They should be plump with bright eyes, flexible feet and smooth claws. The ears of young rabbits will tear easily. Native wild rabbits have much more flavour than those bred for the table or frozen imported rabbit from China. One large rabbit will serve 3–4 people.

Hare. There are two types of hare: English (brown)

and Scotch (blue) hare. The brown is larger and has more flavour. A young hare (leveret) has a smooth coat, small white teeth, soft ears and well-hidden claws. Older hares have a wavy coat, large yellow teeth, an evident cleft in the jaw and protruding blunt claws. Only leverets can be roasted without being marinated to tenderize the meat.

Venison. There are several species of deer in Great Britain, but generally it is only the meat of the red, roe and fallow deer that is eaten. Deer farms are now being developed all over the country and venison is becoming easier to obtain through country butchers and game shops. The quality of 'farmed' deer is normally good, as the age of the animal is known and facilities ensure good preparation of the carcase. Venison joints are available and also sausages and pâté. Being lean, venison freezes well. The best joints for roasting are the haunch and saddle; cutlets and steaks make good frying and the shoulder can be stewed. Game venison generally requires marinating before roasting, but with a good quality of 'farmed' venison, marinating is a matter of personal taste and not necessity.

Plucking, trussing and drawing poultry and game birds
Methods vary little from one type to another, so here is how to go about it:

Plucking. Either hold the bird by its legs, or suspend it by its legs. Start plucking the feathers from the breast. Work with the legs towards you, and pull the feathers away from you. From the breast work down the neck and then towards the tail, and down the legs. Turn the bird over and remove the feathers from the back and the wings. It may be necessary to use pliers on the strong wing-pinion feathers. Remember to keep some of the tail feathers of a pheasant for garnish if the bird is to be roasted.

Drawing. Remove the legs – cut through the skin approximately 2.5 cm (1 inch) below the knee joint, place the cut over the sharp edge of the table or a board, and with a sharp downward movement of the hand, break the leg. It should now be possible to remove the leg sinews by pulling the feet.

Remove the head – place the bird, breast-side down, and cut through the neck skin lengthwise from between the shoulders up to the head. Pull the skin away from the neck and sever the neck and skin just below the head. Cut through the neck by the shoulders, and retain the neck for stock.

Place the bird on its back, loosen the windpipe and food pipe from the neck skin, and remove the crop. If poultry has been starved before killing, the crop should be empty; in game it will usually be full of grain. Place the forefinger inside the neck cavity and loosen the lungs away from the ribs, by working the forefinger backwards and forwards around the rib cage.

Turn to the tail end, and with a sharp knife make a cut between the anus and the parson's nose. Insert the little finger and hook it around the back passage; insert the knife under the loop of the intestine and cut away from the parson's nose – this should cut out the anus completely.

Insert the forefinger into the cavity and loosen the intestines from the walls of the body cavity. Take hold of the gizzard (feels large and firm) and gently pull; the whole of the intestines should be removed, and also the lungs.

Carefully cut the heart away, and the liver. Cut the gall-bladder from the liver, taking care not to break it, otherwise it will impart a bitter flavour. Cut the gizzard away, cut through the muscular casing and remove the sack containing the partially digested food. Retain the heart, liver and gizzard casing with the neck for stock. Wrap the rest in newspaper and dispose of it.

Singe the bird over a clean flame to remove the fine down, then wipe with a clean damp cloth.

Trussing. Place the bird on its back, fold the wings to tuck behind the shoulders, and push the legs forward. With a trussing needle threaded with fine string, pass the needle from one hip joint through the body cavity to the other hip joint. Pass it up the length of one wing, across the back, just below the neck, and down the length of the other wing. Pull the string up tightly and tie the two ends together.

Take another length of string in the needle and pass the needle through the tail-end of the breast bone. Remove the needle, take the two ends of the string over the legs, cross them over the cavity and tie them behind the parson's nose.

Take the flap of neck skin and tuck it under the wings and string across the back.

Trussing variations for game birds. It is usual with game birds to leave the legs and feet on, although the toes should be cut off. Often with pheasant and other larger birds the feet and part of the leg may be removed. The scaly part of the legs should be dipped in boiling water and the scales scraped off.

Traditionally, small game birds such as quail, woodcock and snipe are not drawn. The head should be skinned and the eyes removed. (A woodcock should also have the gizzard removed.) The beak should be twisted around and used like a skewer to truss the bird. During cooking the trail (alimentary canal) turns to liquid and soaks into the toast on which the bird is cooked.

Today, many people prefer to draw and truss these birds as for other game birds.

Jointing poultry and game birds
Place the bird, breast uppermost, tail towards you, and, with a sharp knife, cut through the skin between the leg and the breast; press the leg outwards and downwards, insert the knife in the hip joint, cut around and remove the leg. With a small chicken, the leg may be left as one portion; with a larger bird, it may be divided into two.

Cut down through the breast approximately 2.5 cm (1 inch) in from the wing, and cut the wing off – this ensures a reasonable amount of breast meat on the wing joint. Fillet the breast meat off the carcase. Repeat on the second side. The carcase may be used for making stock.

Pigeons. If acquired in large numbers, it is advisable to use only the breasts. With a sharp knife, cut along the breastbone, skin the breast area and fillet each breast 'steak' away from the carcase or, from the tail end lift the breast bone and, using scissors, cut through the skin and shoulder joints and lift the breast off completely.

Boning out poultry and game birds
Place the bird breast down, and with a sharp knife, cut the skin down the backbone; keeping the knife close to the carcase, carefully fillet the meat away until you reach the leg joint. Ease the knife through the hip joint, and break the leg away from the carcase. Fillet the meat from the leg. Pull the leg completely inside out to remove the bone (for some recipes you can leave the bones in the legs to give a better shape to the finished item).

Continue cutting away the flesh and skin towards the breastbone. Allow the knife to follow the carcase, removing the meat. Take care down the centre of the breastbone that the skin is not cut. Cut the wing off at the joint furthest from the body. Remove the meat from one side of the bird first, then work on the other side.

Read the recipe on page 17 for finishing. The carcase may be used for making stock.

Turkey, goose and pheasant are also ideal for boning out and can be finished in a variety of ways.

Carving poultry and game birds
Carving instructions are given with the recipes for the different types of bird. In each chapter, the basic recipe for each bird (usually a roasting recipe) contains the information you will need.

Paunching and skinning rabbits and hares
Paunching. Rabbits should be paunched (gutted) as soon as they are killed, by making a slit along the length of the belly and removing the intestine and stomach. They may then be hung.

Hares should be hung head down before gutting. A bowl or polythene bag should be placed or hung under the head to catch any blood. This can be used as a liaison to thicken the sauce of, for example, jugged hare (see page 75). A teaspoonful of vinegar added to the blood will prevent it from clotting.

Skinning. Start by removing the lower part of the legs. From the slit along the belly, loosen the skin around the back and peel it off towards the hind legs. Turn the skin of the legs and peel it off rather like removing a stocking.

Pull the skin down over the body and forelegs in a similar way. The head of the rabbit is removed, but the head of a hare is usually left on. The skin should be cut away from the head, and the eyes removed with a sharp knife.

From the liver, remove the gall bladder, taking care not to break it. Reserve the liver, heart and kidney, also the blood which has collected under the membrane of the ribs of the hare. From the hare remove the blue membrane which covers the meat. Rinse the meat well in cold water and dry well.

Jointing rabbits and hares
Remove the hind legs by cutting through the hip joint with a sharp knife. Remove the forelegs by cutting through the shoulder joint. Trim away the flaps of skin attached to the rib cage, and discard. The carcase may be divided in two lengthwise by cutting down the backbone, each half again being cut into 2 or 3 pieces depending on the size of the rabbit or hare. In a hare, the saddle (backbone) is often left whole for roasting. Joint as above, but leave the backbone complete.

Hanging
Hanging times will depend on personal taste and the weather. In warm humid weather, hanging time will be shorter than in cold dry weather. Game birds are hung by the neck, mammals by the hind legs.

Game – availability and hanging times

	Season	Best	Hanging times (in days)
Pheasant	1 Oct to 1 Feb	Nov & Dec	7–10
Partridge	1 Sept to 1 Feb	Oct & Nov	3–5 (young birds) 8 (older birds)
Grouse	12 Aug to 10 Dec	Aug to Oct	7–10
Black game	20 Aug to 10 Dec	Aug to Oct	3–10
Ptarmigan	12 Aug to 10 Dec	Aug to Oct	2–4
Capercaillie	1 Oct to 31 Jan	Nov & Dec	10–14
Wild duck	1 Sept to 31 Jan	Nov & Dec	up to 3
Woodcock	1 Oct to 31 Jan	Nov & Dec	3–5
Snipe	12 Aug to 31 Jan	Nov	3–4
Quail	(Farmed) all year		Little or none
Pigeon	All year		Little or none
Rabbit	All year		3–5
Hare	1 Aug to 28 Feb	Oct onwards	7–10
Venison	1 Aug to 30 Apr	Depends on species & sex	8–10 (red deer) 7 (fallow & roe)
	(Farmed) all year		2–5

Measurements

All spoon measures are level, and eggs are size 2, unless stated otherwise.

Please use either the metric or the imperial measurements; do not mix the two.

American equivalents

	Metric	Imperial	American
Butter, margarine	225 g	8 oz	1 cup
Flour	100 g	4 oz	1 cup
Breadcrumbs, fresh	75 g	3 oz	1¾ cups
Cheese, grated	100 g	4 oz	1¼ cups

An American pint is 16 fl oz compared with the imperial pint of 20 fl oz. A standard American cup measure is considered to hold 8 fl oz.

POULTRY

Poultry can be cooked in hundreds of different and delicious ways. In this chapter chicken, turkey, duck and goose are roasted, casseroled, used in salads and made into soups, loaves and pâtés.

ROAST CHICKEN (1)

Serves 4–6

1 chicken, 1.6–1.8 kg (3½–4 lb)
stuffing of own choice – traditionally
*   parsley and thyme (see page 88)*
100 g (4 oz) dripping
streaky bacon rashers (optional)
1 tbsp plain flour
275 ml (½ pint) chicken stock (see
*   page 91)*

Heat the oven to 220°C (425°F) mark 7. Place the stuffing in the cavity of the bird and, if desired, place the bacon rashers over the breast – this will prevent drying out. Heat the dripping in a roasting tin, and place the bird in it, baste well and place in the oven. Reduce the temperature after 15 minutes to 190°C (375°F) mark 5, and roast for a further 1 hour, or until tender, basting regularly. 15 minutes before the end of cooking, remove the bacon rashers (if used) and sprinkle the breast with a little flour, baste well, and continue cooking.

To test to see if cooked, take a fine skewer, or a cooking knife with a fine point and insert it into the flesh of the thigh. If the juice that comes out is clear, the bird is cooked; if there is any pinkness, continue cooking.

Transfer the bird to a serving dish and keep warm. Remove most of the fat from the roasting tin, place the tin over the heat and stir in the flour; cook for 2–3 minutes, then gradually stir in the stock, bring to the boil and simmer for 3–5 minutes. Strain into a sauceboat.

Serve the chicken with bacon rolls (see page 94) and bread sauce (see page 89).

If time allows, the bird will be much easier to carve if, when cooked, it is placed on the serving dish, covered with foil and several layers of cloth, and allowed to stand for at least 30 minutes. This resting period allows the meat to set.

To carve, hold the bird firmly with a carving fork, insert the carving knife between the leg and the breast, and cut through the skin. Gently press the leg outwards and cut through the joint. Divide the leg into 2 portions. Slice down the breast about 2.5 cm (1 inch) in from the wing joint, and cut through the wing joint – this ensures that a reasonable amount of breast is served with the wing. Carve the rest of the breast into slices. Repeat the process for the second side of the bird.

ROAST CHICKEN (2)

Serves 4–6

1 chicken, 1.6–1.8 kg (3½–4 lb)
2–3 sprigs fresh thyme or rosemary
50 g (2 oz) butter
salt and pepper
275 ml (½ pint) chicken stock (see
  page 91)
1 tsp arrowroot or cornflour

Heat the oven to 200°C (400°F) mark 6. Place the herb with a good nut of butter and seasoning inside the bird, and rub the outside of the bird with the rest of the butter. Place the bird breast side up in a roasting tin with half the stock, cover with buttered paper or foil and place in the oven. Roast for about 1 hour. After the first 15–20 minutes, baste the bird and turn it on to one side. Baste and turn again after another 15–20 minutes; finish off the cooking with the breast side up, removing the paper for the last few minutes to allow the breast to brown. Test to see if the chicken is cooked (see page 15).

Place the bird on a serving dish and keep warm. Add the remaining stock to the roasting tin, and stir well to ensure that all the pan juices are incorporated. Thicken with 1 teaspoonful arrowroot on cornflour mixed with 1 tablespoonful water. Strain into a sauceboat.

Variation
Roasting in a chicken brick: soak the brick in cold water as directed in the instructions. Season the chicken well, inside and out, and place in the cavity either butter and herbs

(as in the recipe above), or for a delicate flavour, place 2 small onions and 1 lemon in the cavity. Place the bird in the brick and cook according to the manufacturer's instructions.

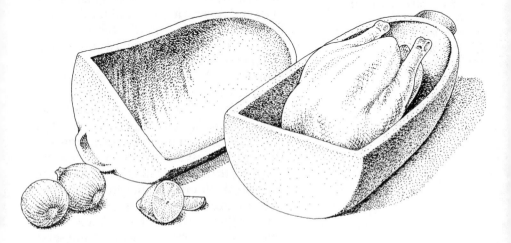

ROAST BONED CHICKEN

Serves about 10 as a buffet dish

1 large chicken, 2.7–3.6 kg (6–8 lb), boned out (see page 11)
700 g (1½ lb) pork sausagemeat
double recipe quantity parsley and thyme stuffing (see page 88)
4–6 lambs' tongues, boiled, skinned and boned

Heat the oven to 200°C (400°F) mark 6. Place the boned out chicken, skin side down, and cover with the sausagemeat. Lay half the stuffing down the centre and place the lambs' tongues on the stuffing; cover with the remaining stuffing.

Bring the sides to the centre and over-sew with fine string. Turn the bird over and re-shape. Weigh the bird. Roast as for method 2 (see opposite).

This is ideal for a buffet; it may be eaten hot or cold, but will slice more easily when cold.

ROAST CHICKEN WITH HONEY

Serves 4–6

1 chicken, 1.6 kg (3½ lb)
salt and pepper
2 oranges
2 cloves
150 ml (¼ pint) dry white wine
150 ml (¼ pint) chicken stock (see
  page 91)
1 tbsp honey
1 tbsp cornflour
orange slices and watercress to
  garnish

Heat the oven to 190°C (375°F) mark 5. Season the chicken well inside, and place one orange, stuck with the cloves, in the cavity. Place in a roasting tin.

Mix the juice of the second orange with the wine, chicken stock and honey and pour the mixture over the chicken. Place in the oven and cover with buttered foil, and roast for approximately 1 hour. After the first 15–20 minutes, baste the bird and turn it on one side. Baste and turn again after another 15–20 minutes. Finish off the cooking with the breast uppermost, and remove the foil for the last few minutes to allow the breast to brown. Test to see if the chicken is cooked (see page 15). Transfer the bird to a serving dish and keep warm.

Measure the pan juices and make up to 275 ml (½ pint) with chicken stock. Mix the cornflour with a little water, and add to the pan juices. Stir until it boils and thickens, strain into a sauceboat and serve separately.

Serve the chicken garnished with orange slices and watercress.

CHICKEN WITH ASPARAGUS

Serves 4–6

1 chicken, 1.6–1.8 kg (3½–4 lb),
  jointed (see page 10)
25 g (1 oz) butter
1 tsp oil
150 ml (¼ pint) chicken stock (see
  page 91)
150 ml (¼ pint) dry white wine
seasoning

Heat the butter and oil in a flameproof casserole, and fry the chicken joints until golden brown. Add the stock, wine and seasoning. Bring to the boil and cover. Simmer gently for 45 minutes, or until the meat is tender.

Meanwhile, make the sauce: melt the butter and gently sauté the sliced mushrooms. Drain the asparagus spears, reserving the liquid. Blend the flour with a

Sauce
25 g (1 oz) butter
100 g (4 oz) button mushrooms,
    sliced
425 g (15 oz) canned asparagus
    spears
1 tsp plain flour
150 ml (¼ pint) single cream
1 tsp Parmesan cheese

little liquid, then add the cream to the flour, and stir well to blend.

When the chicken is cooked, transfer the joints to a serving dish and keep warm. Measure the liquid, and make up to 425 ml (¾ pint) with the asparagus liquid, add the cream mixture and return to the casserole. Bring to the boil and stir until it thickens. Add the mushrooms. Spoon over the chicken pieces and place the asparagus spears at each end of the dish. Sprinkle the sauce with the Parmesan cheese and brown under a hot grill before serving.

SPICY CHICKEN WITH ALMONDS

Serves 6

1 large chicken, 2 kg (4½ lb)
1 tbsp ground coriander
1 tsp freshly ground black pepper
1 tsp ground ginger
½ tsp ground cardamom
½ tsp ground cloves
1 tsp salt
50 g (2 oz) butter, melted

Sauce
50 g (2 oz) butter
350 g (12 oz) onions, finely chopped
    or minced
1 tsp turmeric
150 ml (¼ pint) plain yoghurt
150 ml (¼ pint) single cream
150 ml (¼ pint) double cream
100 g (4 oz) blanched almonds,
    sliced
50 g (2 oz) raisins, chopped

Heat the oven to 200°C (400°F) mark 6. Skin the chicken and prick well all over. Mix together the spices with the salt, and rub into the chicken. Pour the melted butter over. Roast for 1½–1¾ hours (or spit-roast) until the meat is tender, basting occasionally.

Meanwhile, melt the butter in a pan and fry the onion until beginning to soften, then stir in the rest of the ingredients.

When the chicken is half cooked, pour the sauce over, and baste every 15 minutes, for the rest of the cooking time. Transfer the chicken to a serving dish and pour the sauce over.

Serve with plain rice and a green salad.

CHICKEN WITH ORANGE AND TARRAGON

Serves 4–6

*1 chicken, 1.6 kg (3 ½ lb), jointed
(see page 10)*
25 g (1 oz) butter
2 tbsp oil
175 g (6 oz) onion, finely chopped
*4 sprigs fresh tarragon or 1 tsp dried
tarragon*
275 ml (½ pint) fresh orange juice
*275 ml (½ pint) chicken stock (see
page 91)*
seasoning
1 tbsp cornflour or arrowroot
*150 ml (¼ pint) sour cream or
yoghurt*
*chopped fresh tarragon or parsley
and orange slices to garnish*

Heat the oven to 180°C (350°F) mark 4.
Heat the butter and oil in a flameproof
casserole, and gently fry the chicken joints
until golden brown. Transfer them to a
plate. Add the onion to the casserole and fry
gently until soft. Add the tarragon and stir
in the orange juice, chicken stock and salt
and pepper. Bring to the boil, and replace
the chicken joints in the casserole. Cover
and place in the oven to cook for about
1½ hours, or until tender.
   Place the chicken on a serving dish and
keep warm. Blend the cornflour (or
arrowroot) with a little cold water, and add
to the casserole. Bring to the boil, stirring
constantly. Check the seasoning, cool
slightly and stir in the sour cream (or
yoghurt). Coat the chicken pieces and
garnish with orange slices and chopped
tarragon or parsley.

CHICKEN MARENGO

Serves 4–6

*1 chicken, 1.6 kg (3 ½ lb), jointed
(see page 10)*
3 tbsp oil
12 small onions
*225 g (8 oz) fresh tomatoes, skinned
and chopped, or canned tomatoes,
chopped*
3 tbsp tomato purée
1 tbsp plain flour
150 ml (¼ pint) dry white wine
*150 ml (¼ pint) chicken stock (see
page 91)*
100 g (4 oz) button mushrooms
salt and pepper

Heat the oil in a deep frying pan, and gently
fry the chicken joints until golden brown.
Add the onions, and lightly brown them.
Sprinkle in the flour, and cook for
3 minutes. Add the tomatoes and the purée,
together with the wine and the stock. Bring
to the boil. Replace the joints in the pan,
season well and add the mushrooms. Cover
tightly and simmer very slowly for
1–1½ hours or until the chicken is tender.
Check the seasoning. Serve with sauté
potatoes and a green vegetable.

This recipe is also excellent using pheasant,
rabbit, venison, etc., instead of chicken.

COQ AU VIN

Serves 4–6

1 chicken, 1.6 kg (3½ lb), jointed
  (see page 10)
2 tbsp plain flour
seasoning
75 g (3 oz) butter
1 tbsp oil
100–175 g (4–6 oz) piece of fat
  bacon, diced
3–4 tbsp brandy (optional)
bunch of fresh mixed herbs, or a
  bouquet garni
575 ml (1 pint) red wine
12 small onions
12 button mushrooms
croûtes to garnish (see page 93)

Coat the chicken joints in seasoned flour. Heat 25 g (1 oz) of the butter and the oil in a flameproof casserole and fry the diced bacon until crisp; remove the bacon to a plate. Fry the chicken joints until golden brown. Pour the brandy (if used) into a heated ladle. Set the brandy alight and pour it whilst flaming over the chicken. Allow the flame to die out. Add the herbs and the red wine. Cover and simmer for approximately 45 minutes, or until the chicken is tender.

Meanwhile, in another pan, melt the remaining butter, add the onions and fry them lightly. Cover the pan and allow them to cook until soft. Add the mushrooms and cook for 5 minutes more. 15 minutes before the chicken is cooked, add the bacon, onions and mushrooms to the casserole. Serve garnished with croûtes.

CHICKEN WITH TOMATOES

Serves 4

1 chicken, 1.5 kg (3 lb), jointed (see
  page 10)
salt and pepper
50 g (2 oz) butter
2 tbsp oil
175 g (6 oz) onion, chopped
100 g (4 oz) ham, in a thick slice,
  cubed
450 g (1 lb) fresh tomatoes, skinned
  and chopped or canned tomatoes,
  chopped
2 cloves garlic, crushed
6 peppercorns, bruised
1 tsp sugar

Heat the oven to 180°C (350°F) mark 4. Season the chicken joints. Heat the oil and butter in a flameproof casserole and gently fry the chicken joints until evenly browned. Remove to a plate. Place the onion and ham in the casserole and fry gently until the onion starts to soften. Add all the other ingredients, with salt to taste. Cook and stir until a thick sauce is obtained.

Replace the chicken joints in the casserole and spoon the sauce over. Cover the dish tightly and cook in the oven for ¾–1 hour or until the meat is tender.

CHICKEN CACCIATORA

Serves 4–6

1 chicken, 1.6 kg (3½ lb), jointed
  (see page 10)
1 tbsp plain flour, seasoned
3 tbsp oil
1 large onion, chopped
2 cloves garlic (optional), crushed
  with a little salt
1 small green pepper, de-seeded and
  thinly sliced
150 ml (¼ pint) red wine or chicken
  stock (see page 91)
450 g (1 lb) fresh tomatoes, skinned
  and chopped, or 425 g (15 oz)
  canned tomatoes, chopped
1 bouquet garni
50 g (2 oz) button mushrooms, sliced
chopped fresh parsley to garnish

Toss the chicken joints in the seasoned flour. Heat 2 tablespoonfuls of the oil in a flameproof casserole, and fry the joints to a golden brown; transfer them to a plate. Add the remaining oil to the casserole and fry the onion and garlic (if used) until soft. Add the green pepper and fry for 5 minutes. Stir in any remaining flour, add the wine (or stock), the tomatoes and the bouquet garni.

Replace the chicken joints in the pan. Cover and simmer gently for 1 hour or until tender. 20 minutes before the end of cooking, stir in the mushrooms. Check the seasoning.

Serve with generously buttered spaghetti, garnished with chopped parsley.

JAMAICAN CHICKEN CASSEROLE

Serves 4

4 chicken joints
25 g (1 oz) plain flour
1 tsp salt
1 tsp curry powder
1 tsp dry mustard
¼ tsp ground mace
¼ tsp ground marjoram
2 tsp oil
225 g (8 oz) onion, chopped
1 celery stalk, chopped
100 g (4 oz) mushrooms, chopped
150 ml (¼ pint) sweetened orange
  juice
150 ml (¼ pint) chicken stock (see
  page 91)
3 tbsp rum

Heat the oven to 180°C (350°F) mark 4. Mix together the flour, salt and spices, and coat the chicken joints with the mixture.

Heat the oil in a flameproof casserole, and fry the chicken until a golden brown; transfer to a plate. Fry the onion and celery in the casserole until beginning to soften, add the mushrooms and cook for 3–4 minutes. Stir in any remaining flour/spice mixture. Blend in the orange juice and stock and bring to the boil. Add the rum. Replace the chicken joints. Cover tightly and cook in the oven for about 1 hour or until tender.

Serve with rice, or creamed potatoes with buttered spinach. Sliced bananas, sprinkled with lemon juice and topped with sour cream make a good accompaniment.

FRIED CHICKEN PROVENÇALE

Serves 4–6

1 chicken, 1.6 kg (3½ lb)
8 sprigs fresh thyme
8 rashers bacon
50 g (2 oz) butter
2 tbsp oil
175 g (6 oz) onion, finely chopped
450 g (1 lb) fresh tomatoes, skinned
   and chopped, or canned tomatoes,
   chopped
1 tbsp tomato purée
1 tbsp plain flour
1 clove garlic, crushed with salt
275 ml (½ pint) white wine
salt and pepper
slices of French bread, fried, and
   chopped fresh parsley to garnish

Joint the chicken into 8 portions (see page 10). Lay a sprig of thyme on each, and wrap in bacon. Tie with string.

Heat the butter and oil in a large deep frying pan, and fry the chicken parcels to a golden brown. Remove from the pan to a plate. Add the onion to the fats in the pan and fry gently until soft. Stir in the tomatoes and purée, and cook for a few minutes. Stir in the flour and garlic and cook for a further 2–3 minutes. Add the wine and some seasoning. Bring to the boil, and replace the chicken joints. Cover and cook gently for 30–40 minutes, or until the chicken is tender. Remove the string.

Arrange the joints on a dish, skim the sauce, adjust the seasoning, and spoon over the joints. Garnish with slices of fried French bread and chopped parsley.

CELEBRATION CHICKEN

Serves about 8 as a buffet dish

1 chicken, 1.6 kg (3½ lb), cooked
   and cut into pieces when cold
25 g (1 oz) butter
175 g (6 oz) onion, chopped
1 tbsp curry powder
150 ml (¼ pint) well-flavoured
   chicken stock (see page 91)
2 tsp tomato purée
2 tbsp lemon juice
2 tbsp sieved apricot jam
1 recipe quantity mayonnaise (see
   page 92)
3–4 tbsp single cream
lettuce leaves to garnish

Melt the butter in a saucepan, and gently fry the onion until soft. Stir in the curry powder and cook for 2–3 minutes. Add the chicken stock, tomato purée, lemon juice and apricot jam. Bring to the boil and ensure they are well mixed. Allow to go cold. Mix with the mayonnaise and cream, and combine with the chicken.

Line a large serving bowl with lettuce leaves and pile the chicken in the bowl.

CHICKEN IN A CREAM SAUCE

Serves 4–6

1 boiling fowl
1 litre (1¾ pints) water
1 onion
1 bayleaf
salt and pepper
100 g (4 oz) mushrooms, sliced, and
  sautéed in 25 g (1 oz) butter
25 g (1 oz) butter
25 g (1 oz) plain flour
275 ml (½ pint) chicken stock (see
  page 91)
150 ml (¼ pint) single cream
2 egg yolks
½ tsp ground nutmeg
1 tsp lemon juice

Place the boiling fowl in a pan with the water, onion, bay leaf and seasoning. Cover and cook until tender (2–3 hours). Allow to cool slightly. Remove the bones and skin, and cut the meat into medium-sized pieces. Place in a serving dish and sprinkle the sautéed mushrooms over.

For the sauce – melt the butter in a pan, add the flour and cook for 1 minute. Gradually add the chicken stock, and bring to the boil, stirring constantly. Season to taste. Boil for 3–4 minutes, and allow to cool slightly. Mix the cream and egg yolks together in a basin and add to the sauce with the nutmeg and juice. Reheat without boiling and pour over the chicken pieces. Serve hot or cold.

The liquid that the bird was cooked in may be boiled to reduce in volume, and concentrate the flavour. It must be well skimmed. This may be used for the stock required in the dish, and the remainder used as the basis of a soup.

SUFFOLK CHICKEN CASSEROLE

Serves 4–6

1 boiling fowl
1 onion
1 carrot
1 bay leaf
salt and pepper
1 litre (1¾ pints) water
25 g (1 oz) butter
1 tbsp oil
2 medium onions, thinly sliced
175 g (6 oz) mushrooms, sliced
425 ml (¾ pint) dry cider
2 tbsp Worcestershire sauce
1 tbsp cornflour
150 g (5 oz) natural yoghurt
2 medium apples to garnish

Place the boiling fowl in a pan with the onion, carrot, bay leaf, seasoning and water. Cover and simmer gently until the meat is cooked (2–3 hours). Allow to cool slightly. Skin the bird, and remove the meat from the bones. Cut the meat into pieces and place them in a flameproof casserole.

Heat the oil and butter in a pan and gently fry the onions until soft; add the mushrooms and cook for 4–5 minutes. Place the onions and mushrooms on top of the chicken pieces. Add the cider, Worcestershire sauce and salt and pepper. Cover tightly and simmer gently for ¾–1 hour.

Blend the cornflour with a little water in a basin, add 2–3 tablespoonfuls of the cooking liquid, mix, pour into the casserole and bring to the boil. Remove from the heat and stir in the yoghurt. Check the seasoning.

Meanwhile, core the apples and cut into 5-mm (¼-inch) thick rings. Fry these gently in a little butter and use to garnish the casserole.

COLD CHICKEN SALAD

Serves about 8 as a buffet dish

*1 chicken, 1.6 kg (3½ lb), cooked,
and cut into small pieces when
cold*
*100 g (4 oz) mushrooms, sliced and
sautéed in 25 g (1 oz) butter*
4 eggs, hard-boiled and chopped
*4 rashers bacon, crisply fried and
chopped*
*425 g (15 oz) canned sweetcorn,
drained*
1 small packet frozen peas, cooked
1 red pepper, chopped
50 g (2 oz) walnuts, chopped
salt and pepper
*150–275 ml (¼–½ pint)
mayonnaise (see page 92), or
vinaigrette dressing (see page 92)*
1 tbsp lemon juice
*asparagus spears, sliced cucumber
and paprika pepper to garnish*

Prepare all the ingredients and when they
are cold, combine them together in a large
bowl, with the lemon juice and mayonnaise
(or vinaigrette). Pile on a large serving dish
and garnish with the asparagus spears and
cucumber slices; a light sprinkling of
paprika pepper will give extra colour.
Serve with a rice salad and a green salad.

COCK-A-LEEKIE SOUP

Serves 4

1 boiling fowl
4 medium leeks
*bunch of fresh mixed herbs or
1 bouquet garni*
6 peppercorns
1 tsp salt
50 g (2 oz) long grain rice

Place the boiling fowl in a large saucepan.
Prepare the leeks and cut into 5-cm (2-inch)
lengths. Add to the pan with the herbs,
peppercorns and salt; add sufficient water to
almost cover the bird. Cover, bring to the
boil, remove any scum and simmer for
approximately 2 hours or until the bird is
tender.
Remove the bird from the pan and cut the
flesh from the carcase. Cut the flesh into
bite-size pieces and return to the pan with
the rice. Bring to the boil, and simmer a
further 20 minutes or until the rice is soft.
Check the seasoning before serving.

SIMPLE CHICKEN SOUP

Serves 3–4

1 chicken carcase, plus giblets, if
   available
1 medium onion, chopped
2 medium carrots, chopped
1 stick celery, sliced
1 matchbox-sized piece swede,
   chopped
bunch of fresh mixed herbs, or
   1 bouquet garni
6 peppercorns
salt
beurre manié (see page 92)
double cream and chopped chives to
   garnish

Place the chicken carcase, giblets, prepared vegetables, herbs and seasoning in a large saucepan. Cover with water. Bring to the boil, remove any scum, cover and simmer gently for approximately 1½ hours. Remove the carcase and the herbs. Sieve or liquidize the contents of the pan and thicken with beurre manié. Check the seasoning. Add any meat from the carcase, finely shredded, bring to the boil and simmer for 3–4 minutes.

Serve in individual bowls with a swirl of cream and a few chopped chives.

CHICKEN LIVER PÂTÉ

225 g (8 oz) chicken livers
100 g (4 oz) butter
1 shallot, finely chopped
1 clove garlic, finely chopped
seasoning
1 tbsp brandy
good pinch of mixed dried herbs
clarified butter

Remove any sinews from the livers. Melt 25 g (1 oz) butter in a frying pan, and cook the onion and garlic until soft. Add the livers and sauté briskly (about 10–12 minutes) until the liver is firm to the touch.

Cool the liver, then rub through a fine sieve, mince, or liquidize. Cream the remaining butter and beat into the liver mixture. Season well, and add the brandy and herbs. Place in a china pot, or in small cocottes. Smooth over the top and cover with clarified butter. Store in the refrigerator, and use as required.

Clarified butter is butter which has been 'cleared' by heating until it foams, and then by skimming and straining off the clear yellow oil, leaving the milk solids behind.

ROAST TURKEY (Slow Method)

See page 5 for servings

1 turkey
stuffing(s) of own choice (see
pages 85–88)
50 g (2 oz) butter or dripping, or
225 g (8 oz) streaky bacon
plain flour
giblet gravy (see page 91)
bread sauce (see page 89)
cranberry sauce (see page 89)
sausages
bacon rolls (see page 94)

Heat the oven to 170°C (325°F) mark 3.
Prepare the stuffings. A double quantity of
the recipe will be required for the cavity.
The neck and cavity may both be stuffed.
Weigh the bird after stuffing to calculate the
cooking time.

Either smear the breast with fat, and
completely wrap in foil, or cover the breast
with streaky bacon. Place the bird in a
roasting tin and cook.

Under 6.3 kg (14 lb), allow 45 minutes
per kg (20 minutes per lb) and 30 minutes
over (3 hours 50 minutes for a 4.5-kg/10-lb
bird).

Over 6.3 kg (14 lb), allow 35–40 minutes
per kg (15–18 minutes per lb) and
15 minutes over (approximately 5½ hours
for a 9-kg/20-lb bird).

45 minutes before the end of cooking,
open up the foil or remove the bacon
rashers. Sprinkle lightly with flour,
continue the cooking and allow the breast
to brown.

To test if cooking is finished, place a
skewer into the thickest part of the
drumstick: if it goes in easily and no liquid
runs out, cooking is complete.

Allow 20–30 minutes for dishing up.
During this time the bird may be placed on
a serving dish, covered with foil, and then
covered with several clean tea-towels or a
heavy cloth. This keeps the bird hot, and
allows the meat to 'relax' thus making
carving much easier. The bird can stand
like this for up to 1 hour, meaning therefore
that the oven is at liberty for roasting
potatoes, and preparing other
accompaniments for dinner. Use the pan
juices for the giblet gravy.

The traditional accompaniments to turkey are giblet gravy (see page 91), bread sauce (see page 89), cranberry sauce (see page 89), and sometimes sausages or bacon rolls (see page 94). Chestnuts are often used either in a stuffing, or served with Brussels sprouts; they may also be puréed and added to the gravy to make it richer.

To carve, cut through the skin between the body and a leg, then gently ease the leg away from the body, pressing the leg down towards the plate. This enables the knife to be put through the joint at the top of the thigh, thereby removing the leg completely. Carve the breast by slicing from the breast bone towards the wing. In the case of a small bird, it is usual to serve either a drumstick or a thigh from the leg together with slices of breast meat for one portion. With a larger bird, the leg meat is sliced off and served without the bone.

ROAST TURKEY (Quick Method)

See page 5 for servings

1 turkey
stuffing(s) of own choice (see pages
*   85–88)*
350 g (12 oz) streaky bacon rashers
100 g (4 oz) butter or dripping
plain flour
giblet gravy (see page 91)
bread sauce (see page 89)
cranberry sauce (see page 89)
sausages
bacon rolls (see page 94)

Heat the oven to 220°C (425°F) mark 7. Prepare the stuffings (see note on page 28). Cover the breast with the streaky bacon. Heat the fat in a roasting tin, place the bird in the tin, baste well, and place in the oven. After 20 minutes reduce the heat to 190°C (375°F) mark 5. The bird should be regularly basted throughout cooking.

Under 6.3 kg (14 lb), allow 35 minutes per kg (15 minutes per lb) and 15 minutes over (approximately 2¾ hours for a 4.5-kg/10-lb bird).

Over 6.4 kg (14 lb), allow 23 minutes per kg (10 minutes per lb) and 10 minutes over (approximately 3½ hours for a 9-kg/20-lb bird). Finish the bird as on page 28.

MOIST ROAST TURKEY

See page 5 for servings

1 turkey (not exceeding
*   6.3 kg/14 lb)*
575 ml (1 pint) turkey or chicken
*   stock (see page 91)*
75–100 g (3–4 oz) butter
stuffing(s) of own choice (see pages
*   85–88)*

Heat the oven to 220°C (425°F) mark 7. After 15–20 minutes cooking time, reduce the heat to 190°C (375°F) mark 5. Allow 35 minutes per kg (15 minutes per lb) and 15 minutes over (approximately 2¾ hours for a 4.5-kg/10-lb bird).

Melt the butter in the hot stock. Place the turkey in a roasting tin with one side of the breast down. Pour the hot liquid over it and place the tin in the oven. Baste regularly with the liquid during cooking. After about one-third of the cooking time, remove the tin from the oven, turn the bird onto its other side and continue cooking. After two-thirds of the cooking time, turn the bird onto its back, so that the breast can brown. Test to see if cooking is complete (see page 28). The basting liquid can be used for gravy.

WESSEX TURKEY

Serves 4

1 turkey leg (thigh and drumstick)
2 medium onions
salt
275 ml (½ pint) water
100 g (4 oz) cooked ham or bacon
50 g (2 oz) butter
1 tbsp plain flour
150 ml (¼ pint) dry cider
pepper
croûtes (see page 93)
chopped parsley to garnish

Place the turkey joints in a pan with one of the onions, quartered, ½ teaspoon salt, and 275 ml (½ pint) water. Bring to the boil, cover and simmer for ¾–1 hour, or until tender. Lift out the meat onto a plate, remove the skin and bone, and cut the meat into large pieces.

Strain the stock, and reserve it. Chop the cooked onion. Cut the ham or bacon into 1-cm (½-inch) strips. Slice the second onion, and fry until softened in the butter. Add the flour and cook for 2 minutes. Gradually stir in the cider and reserved stock. Bring to the boil, add the meats and the other onion, season to taste, and simmer for 7 minutes. Pour into a serving dish and garnish with croûtes and chopped parsley.

TURKEY SAUTÉ ANNETTE

Serves 4

1 tbsp cooking oil
25 g (1 oz) butter
2 small turkey legs (thigh and
drumstick)
1 medium onion, chopped
1 tbsp plain flour
575 ml (1 pint) chicken stock (see
page 91) or stock cube and water
275 ml (½ pint) white wine
salt and pepper
2 tsp chopped fresh chervil
2 tsp chopped fresh tarragon
1 tbsp chopped fresh parsley
1 tbsp lemon juice
chopped fresh parsley and strips of
pimento to garnish

Melt the oil and butter in a sauté pan, add the turkey joints and fry until golden brown. Remove the joints. Lightly fry the chopped onion, add the flour and cook for 2 minutes. Gradually stir in the stock and wine, bring to the boil, add seasoning, replace the turkey joints in the pan and add the chervil, tarragon, parsley and lemon juice. Bring to the boil, cover and simmer gently for approximately 1 hour or until the meat is tender.

Place the turkey joints in an oval dish, check the seasoning of the sauce, then pour it over the joints. Garnish with strips of pimento and chopped parsley.

MARINATED TURKEY

Serves 6–8

Marinade
3 bay leaves
3 cloves garlic
4 peppercorns
1 medium onion, sliced
¼ tsp salt
*575 ml (1 pint) white wine or white
wine and water, or white wine
and white wine vinegar*

*1 turkey approx 4 kg (9 lb), jointed
(see page 10)*
3 tbsp cooking oil
2 large onions, sliced
*2–6 cloves of garlic, according to
taste*
2 tomatoes, skinned and chopped
4 peppercorns
2 cloves
½ tsp ground cinnamon
salt

Mix together the ingredients for the
marinade. Place the turkey in a deep dish,
and pour the marinade over; leave at least
4 hours, or overnight if possible. Turn the
joints occasionally.

Remove the joints from the marinade and
dry well. Heat the oil in a heavy saucepan or
casserole, fry the turkey pieces until lightly
browned, and remove from the pan. Add
the sliced onion and fry gently until soft.
Crush the garlic cloves and add to the
onion. Add the remaining ingredients.
Replace the turkey pieces in the pan, and
pour over the strained marinade. Cover the
pan tightly and cook over a low heat for
approximately 2½ hours. Alternatively, if
in a casserole, it may be cooked in the oven
at 150°C (300°F) mark 2.

When cooked, test the seasoning. If
desired, the sauce may be thickened with a
little slaked cornflour.

CARIBBEAN TURKEY

Serves 4

450 g (1 lb) white turkey meat
2 tbsp plain flour
salt and pepper
1 tbsp cooking oil
25 g (1 oz) butter
450 g (1 lb) canned apricot halves
2 tbsp Worcestershire sauce
2 tbsp vinegar
2 tbsp demerara sugar
2 tbsp lemon juice
150 ml (¼ pint) water
225 g (8 oz) long grain rice

Cut the turkey meat into 2.5-cm (1-inch) cubes. Place the flour, salt and pepper in a large polythene bag, add the turkey pieces and toss well.

Place the oil and butter in a flameproof casserole and heat. Add the coated turkey pieces and fry until brown.

Drain the apricot halves, reserve a few for the garnish and coarsely chop the remainder. Reserve the juice, and mix 150 ml (¼ pint) of it with the Worcestershire sauce, vinegar, demerara sugar, lemon juice and water.

Add any remaining flour to the turkey pieces and add the liquids to the pan. Stir gently and bring to the boil, add the chopped apricots, cover and simmer gently for 45 minutes, or until the meat is tender.

Meanwhile cook the long grain rice. Dry the rice, and place in a ring around a large serving dish. Keep warm. When the turkey is tender, check the seasoning and pour the mixture into the centre of the rice. Garnish with the remaining apricots.

TURKEY DIVAN

Serves 4

450 g (1 lb) frozen broccoli
700 g (1½ lb) potatoes, cooked and
    mashed
25 g (1 oz) butter
350 g (12 oz) cooked turkey, sliced
1 can condensed chicken soup
2 tbsp dry sherry, or dry white wine
50 g (2 oz) Cheddar cheese, finely
    grated

Cook the broccoli in boiling salted water. Meanwhile pipe a bed of mashed potato into the centre of a warmed, flat, fireproof dish. Keep warm. Drain the broccoli and arrange around the potato; dot with butter. Place the turkey slices on top of the potato.

Heat the soup undiluted in a saucepan, add the sherry or wine, and pour over the turkey, leaving most of the broccoli uncovered. Sprinkle the sauce with grated cheese, reheat and brown under a hot grill.

SHERRIED TURKEY

Serves 4

25 g (1 oz) butter
1 tbsp cooking oil
450 g (1 lb) turkey joints (leg or wing)
1 small onion, chopped
50 g (2 oz) lean bacon, chopped
50 g (2 oz) mushrooms, chopped
1 tbsp plain flour
salt and pepper
275 ml (½ pint) stock (see page 91)
3 tbsp dry sherry
chopped fresh parsley to garnish

Heat the butter and oil in a heavy pan, add the turkey pieces and gently fry until golden brown. Remove the turkey from the pan.

Add the onion and bacon and fry until the onion is soft, add the mushrooms and cook for 3 minutes. Stir in the flour and seasoning. Gradually add the stock, stirring continuously; bring to the boil, add the sherry, replace the turkey pieces, cover and cook for approximately 45 minutes or until the meat is cooked. Check the seasoning; bring the sauce back to the boil. Pour into a shallow oval dish and garnish with chopped parsley.

TURKEY WITH BABY DUMPLINGS

Serves 4

575 ml (1 pint) béchamel sauce (see page 89)
450 g (1 lb) cold turkey
1 hard-boiled egg, chopped
1–2 tsp chopped capers
chopped fresh parsley to garnish

Dumplings
75 g (3 oz) self-raising flour
pinch of salt
35 g (1½ oz) shredded suet
1 tsp chopped fresh parsley and ½ tsp chopped fresh thyme or 1 tsp mixed dried herbs
3 tbsp water

Make the béchamel sauce, cut the turkey into bite-sized pieces and place in the saucepan with the sauce; heat gently. Stir in the egg and capers.

Make the dumplings by sieving together the flour and salt into a bowl; add the suet and herbs. Mix with water to make a soft, but mouldable, consistency. Divide into 8, and shape each into a dumpling. Drop carefully into fast boiling water and cook for 7–10 minutes. Lift out carefully; place in the sauce, and cook for 2–3 minutes. Serve sprinkled with parsley.

TURKEY TETRAZZINI

Serves 4

225 g (8 oz) spaghetti
1 tbsp cooking oil
3 tbsp strips of streaky bacon
1 large onion, sliced
25 g (1 oz) plain flour
275 ml (½ pint) stock (see page 91)
1 tsp concentrated tomato purée
1 green pepper and 1 red pepper,
    seeded, cut into strips and
    blanched
100 g (4 oz) small mushrooms,
    quartered
350 g (12 oz) cooked turkey, cut into
    strips
Parmesan cheese to sprinkle

Cook the spaghetti in a large pan in fast boiling salted water, until tender (approximately 15 minutes). Drain, and arrange around the edge of a warmed flat serving dish.

Meanwhile heat the oil, and gently fry the onion and bacon, until the onion is soft. Add the flour and cook for 2 minutes. Stir in the stock and tomato purée. Continue stirring and bring to the boil. Add the peppers, mushrooms, and turkey. Season to taste. Bring slowly to the boil, cover and simmer for 10 minutes.

Spoon into the centre of the spaghetti and sprinkle with Parmesan cheese.

DEVILLED TURKEY JOINTS

Serves 4

4 turkey leg or wing joints
1 tsp curry powder
2 tbsp mustard powder
2 tsp Worcestershire sauce
salt and pepper
a few drops of tabasco sauce
    (optional)

Remove the skin from turkey joints, and score the flesh. Mix a sauce with the rest of the ingredients, and cover each joint thoroughly. Either grill the joints slowly until cooked, or bake in the oven at 180°C (350°F) mark 4, until brown and the meat is tender.

Serve with creamed potatoes and Brussels sprouts.

TURKEY LOAF

Serves 4

350 g (12 oz) cooked turkey, minced
100 g (4 oz) fresh breadcrumbs
½ tsp dry mustard
1 medium onion, minced
75 g (3 oz) mushrooms, chopped
½ tsp celery salt
2 tbsp chopped fresh parsley
2 eggs, beaten
150 ml (¼ pint) milk
1 tsp Worcestershire sauce
salt and pepper

Heat the oven to 180°C (350°F) mark 4. Into a large bowl place the turkey, breadcrumbs, mustard, onion, mushrooms, celery salt and parsley. Mix well together. Add the beaten eggs, milk and Worcestershire sauce. Mix again, ensuring all the ingredients are well blended. Season to taste. Place the mixture in a well-greased 900-g (2-lb) loaf tin. Bake in the oven, until firm, for about 1 hour. Leave in the tin for 5 minutes before turning out onto a serving dish. Serve hot or cold.

TURKEY WITH AVOCADO SALAD

Serves 4

2 avocados
fresh orange juice
½ small red pepper and ½ green
  pepper, de-seeded
225 g (8 oz) cooked turkey, diced
1–2 tsp Worcestershire sauce
2–3 tbsp mayonnaise (see page 92)
salt and pepper

Peel and core the avocados, slice, and arrange in overlapping slices in a circle on a serving plate. Brush with orange juice.

From each of the peppers, reserve a few fine slices for garnish, and finely chop the remainder.

Mix the turkey with the chopped peppers, Worcestershire sauce and mayonnaise. Season to taste. Pile the mixture in the centre of the avocado slices. Garnish with the reserved slices of peppers.

Chill well. Serve with a watercress salad.

TURKEY SALAD

Serves 4

225 g (8 oz) cooked turkey, diced
225 g (8 oz) cooked long grain rice
½ red pepper and ½ green pepper,
  de-seeded and finely sliced
2 tbsp cooked sweetcorn kernels
25 g (1 oz) walnuts, chopped
25 g (1 oz) sultanas
vinaigrette dressing (see page 92)
sliced cucumber to garnish

Mix together the turkey, rice, peppers, sweetcorn, walnuts and sultanas. Add sufficient vinaigrette dressing to moisten.

Pile onto a plate, and garnish with a ring of finely sliced cucumber.

TURKEY AND HAM SALAD

Serves 3–4

100 g (4 oz) cooked turkey, diced
100 g (4 oz) cooked ham, diced
150 g (6 oz) cooked long grain rice
3–4 tbsp fresh or canned pineapple,
  diced
3–4 tbsp melon, diced
2 eating apples, cored and sliced
4–6 tbsp mayonnaise (see page 92)
lettuce, tomato and cucumber to
  garnish

Mix together the turkey, ham, rice, pineapple, melon and apple. Fold in the mayonnaise.

Arrange the lettuce on a serving dish, and pile the salad on top. Garnish with sliced or quartered tomatoes and sliced cucumber.

ROAST DUCK WITH ORANGE SAUCE

Serves 4

1 oven-ready duckling, about 2 kg
    (4½ lb)
salt and pepper
1 medium carrot, sliced
1 medium onion, sliced
4 navel oranges
150 ml (¼ pint) port or Madeira
2–3 tbsp Cointreau or Grand
    Marnier
a few drops of lemon juice (if
    necessary)
25 g (1 oz) butter, softened

Sauce
3 tbsp granulated sugar
3 tbsp red wine vinegar
275 ml (¾ pint) duck stock, using
    the giblets (see page 91)
1 tbsp arrowroot
2 tbsp port or Madeira
orange peel

Heat the oven to 220°C (425°F) mark 7. Season the cavity of the duck. Remove the zest from the oranges with a zester (or with a potato peeler then cut into julienne strips); simmer in 575 ml (1 pint) water for 15 minutes. Drain. Place one-third of the zest in the bird's cavity.

Prick the skin around the thighs, back and lower breast. Place in a roasting tin with the vegetables. Roast in the oven for 15 minutes, reduce the heat to 180°C (350°F) mark 4, and turn the duck on its side. After 30 minutes, turn the duck onto its other side. Remove any accumulated fat occasionally. 15 minutes before the end of roasting time, turn the duck on its back, and sprinkle with salt. (Total cooking time – 1¼ to 1½ hours).

Whilst the bird is roasting, prepare the sauce. Place the vinegar and sugar in a pan and heat to form a caramel. Remove from the heat and stir in 150 ml (¼ pint) of the stock. Simmer gently to dissolve the caramel; add the remaining stock. Blend the arrowroot with the port or Madeira, and add to the stock, with the remaining orange zest. Stir, bring to the boil, and simmer for 3–4 minutes until the sauce clears. Adjust the seasoning.

Remove the remaining skin from the oranges, and divide into segments.

When the duck is cooked, remove it from the roasting tin, place on a serving dish and keep warm. Remove surplus fat from the roasting tin, add the port or Madeira and boil, incorporating the pan juices; reduce the liquid to 2–3 tablespoonfuls. Strain into the prepared sauce; bring to the simmer. Add Cointreau or Grand Marnier to taste (correcting oversweetness with lemon juice). Just before serving, and away from the heat, stir in the butter.

Garnish the duck with the orange segments and spoon a little sauce over; serve the rest separately.

Ducks are awkward to carve, so carving is best carried out in the kitchen. Cut straight through the breastbone and back, using scissors or game shears to cut through the bone. Lay each half cut side down, and make a slanting cut through the breast, separating the wing and the leg, ensuring that each piece has some breast.

ROAST DUCK WITH BAKED APPLES

Serves 6

1 duck, 2.25–2.7 kg (5–6 lb)
salt
6 medium-sized cooking apples

Stuffing
4 large onions
10 fresh sage leaves, chopped
100 g (4 oz) fresh breadcrumbs
25 g (1 oz) butter or margarine
salt and pepper
1 egg, beaten

Heat the oven to 200°C (400°F) mark 6. Prepare the stuffing – boil the onions for 10 minutes, then chop finely. Add the sage, breadcrumbs, butter and seasoning. Bind together with the beaten egg.

Stuff the duck and truss it (see page 9). Sprinkle the duck with salt and prick the skin around the legs and the back. Place in a roasting tin in the oven, and when the fat starts running, baste well every 20 minutes until the bird is cooked. Roast for 35 minutes per kg (15 minutes per lb) and 15 minutes over.

Peel and core the apples and place in the roasting tin with the duck, 45 minutes before the end of cooking. Serve the duck on a shallow plate, surrounded by the apples.

Variation
Stuff each apple with well-seasoned sausagemeat, and cook as before.

DUCKLING PROVENÇAL STYLE

Serves 4

1.8-kg (4-lb) duckling, cut into
    4 joints
2 tbsp plain flour
salt and pepper
1 tbsp oil
25 g (1 oz) butter
225 g (8 oz) onion, chopped
2 cloves garlic, crushed
1 green pepper, de-seeded and
    chopped
2 tomatoes, skinned, pipped and
    chopped
1 tbsp tomato purée
2 tsp sugar
200 ml (7 fl oz) stock (see page 91)
200 ml (7 fl oz) white wine
2–3 stuffed olives, sliced
225 g (8 oz) long grain rice
lemon slices to garnish

Heat the oven to 150°C (300°F) mark 2. Mix the flour and salt and pepper in a polythene bag, add the duckling joints and shake well to ensure the joints are well coated. Heat the oil and butter in a flameproof casserole, and fry the joints until evenly browned, then transfer them to a plate.

Add the onion to the pan and fry gently to soften. Add the crushed garlic, the pepper and the tomatoes, and fry for 5–6 minutes. Add the tomato purée and sugar. Stir in the stock and wine, bring to the boil, replace the duckling joints and add the sliced olives. Cover tightly and place in the oven. Cook for 1½–1¾ hours or until the meat is tender.

Cook the rice. Remove the duckling from the oven and check the seasoning. Skim off excess fat. Serve with the rice garnished with lemon slices.

DUCK WITH SPICY ORANGE SALAD

Serves 4

1.8-kg (4-lb) duck
salt

Stuffing
450 g (1 lb) onions, chopped
150 ml (¼ pint) water
salt and pepper
75 g (3 oz) fresh breadcrumbs
2 tsp chopped fresh sage
50 g (2 oz) margarine

Spicy orange salad
2 tbsp oil
1 large onion, sliced and separated
into rings
4 oranges
¼ tsp cayenne pepper
2 tbsp stuffed green olives, sliced
1 tbsp finely chopped fresh parsley

Heat the oven to 230°C (450°F) mark 8. To make the stuffing, place the onions in a saucepan with the water and cook for 10 minutes. Season well. Strain, reserving the liquid, and mix with the breadcrumbs, sage and margarine, adding sufficient of the onion stock to moisten. Cool, then stuff the cavity of the duck, sprinkle the bird with salt, and prick around the legs and back.

Place in a roasting tin, and roast for 30 minutes. Reduce the oven temperature to 190°C (375°F) mark 5, and cook for another hour, or until tender. Transfer to a serving dish.

While the duck is cooking, make the salad. Heat the oil in a frying pan and fry the onion rings for approximately 10 minutes, but do not brown. Lift out of the pan and drain on absorbent paper.

Cut the peel from the oranges, ensuring that all the pith is removed, and slice them into rings. Place the orange slices in a shallow dish, arrange the onion rings on top, and sprinkle with the cayenne pepper and the sliced olives. Chill for at least 30 minutes before serving. Serve sprinkled with the parsley.

BRAISED DUCK

Serves 4

1 duck, cut into 4 joints
seasoning
1 tbsp oil
25 g (1 oz) butter
1 large onion, chopped
2 medium carrots, chopped
1 rasher bacon, chopped
1 tbsp plain flour
150 ml (¼ pint) red wine
275 ml (½ pint) stock (see page 91)
1 orange
bunch of fresh herbs – bayleaf,
  savoury, sage, parsley
50 g (2 oz) mushrooms, sliced
orange slices and watercress to
  garnish

Heat the oven to 170°C (325°F) mark 3. Season the duck joints well. Heat the oil and butter in a flameproof casserole, and lightly brown the duck joints. Transfer them to a plate. Add the onion, carrot and bacon to the casserole and fry gently until the vegetables begin to soften. Add the flour and cook for 1–2 minutes. Stir in the wine and stock and bring to boil. Grate the orange rind and add it to the stock with the herbs.

Replace the duck joints in the casserole. Cover tightly and cook in the oven for about 1¼ hours. Add the juice of the orange and the mushrooms. Continue cooking for a further 30 minutes or until the meat is tender. Remove the joints to a serving dish and keep warm. Strain the sauce, skimming off any excess fat. Adjust the seasoning, and pour the sauce over the joints. Garnish with orange slices and watercress.

This recipe is suitable for an older duck.

ROAST DUCKLING WITH PEACHES

Serves 4

1 plump duckling, 1.8–2 kg
  (4–4½ lb)
salt
575 ml (1 pint) espagnole sauce,
  using the duck giblets (see
  page 90)
1 large can peach halves
120 ml (4 fl oz) dry sherry
2 tbsp peach brandy

Heat the oven to 200°C (400°F) mark 6. Prepare the stuffing – melt the butter in a pan, add the onion and cook gently until softened. Place all the ingredients in a bowl and mix well. Stuff the cavity of the bird. Salt the outside of the bird, and prick the legs and back. Weigh the bird and cook (see page 39).

Drain the peach halves. 10 minutes before the end of cooking time, place one peach half per person in the roasting tin to heat through.

Stuffing
100 g (4 oz) onion, finely chopped
50 g (2 oz) butter
25 g (1 oz) walnuts, chopped
50 g (2 oz) seeded raisins, chopped
rind and juice of ½ lemon
225 g (8 oz) pork sausagemeat

Chop the remaining peach halves. When the duck is ready, place it on a serving dish with the peach halves and keep warm. Remove the surplus fat from the roasting tin, and add a little hot water to the tin to de-glaze it. Strain the liquid into the previously prepared sauce, add the sherry, peach brandy, chopped peaches and 3 tablespoonfuls peach juice. Heat gently, adjust the seasoning and pour into a sauce-boat.

DUCKLING WITH BLACK CHERRIES

Serves 4

1.8–2-kg (4–4½-lb) duckling
salt

Stuffing
25 g (1 oz) butter
1 medium onion, chopped
100 g (4 oz) walnuts or cashews,
    chopped
100 g (4 oz) fresh breadcrumbs
1 tbsp chopped fresh parsley
1 tsp chopped fresh sage
1 tsp chopped fresh thyme
pinch of ground cinnamon
seasoning
grated rind of 1 lemon, juice of
    ½ lemon
beaten egg

Sauce
450 g (1-lb) canned black cherries
    (stoned)
3 tbsp red wine vinegar
2 tsp arrowroot or cornflour

Heat the oven to 200°C (400°F) mark 6. To make the stuffing, heat the butter and gently fry the onion until it is soft; lightly fry the nuts to a golden brown. Place all the ingredients in a bowl and mix well, adding sufficient egg to bind. Place the stuffing in the cavity of the duck, and truss the duck.

Sprinkle the duck well with salt and prick around the legs and back. Weigh the duck and cook (see page 39).

When the duck is cooked, place it on a serving dish and keep warm. Remove the excess fat from the roasting tin, add a little hot water to the tin to de-glaze. Place this in a measure, add the red wine vinegar and strained cherry juice, and make up to 275 ml (½ pint) with water. Blend the arrowroot or cornflour with a little cold water, add the juice mixture, place in a pan, and bring to the boil stirring constantly. Add the cherries, and cook gently for 2–3 minutes. Pour into a sauce-boat.

Garnish the duck with watercress and serve with duchesse potatoes.

SALMIS OF DUCK

Serves 4

1 duckling
salt

Sauce
25 g (1 oz) butter
duck giblets
1 small onion, diced
1 small carrot, diced
50 g (2 oz) bacon, cut in strips
1 tbsp plain flour
seasoning
bunch of fresh mixed herbs or
    bouquet garni
275 ml (½ pint) water
150 ml (½ pint) red wine

Garnish
12 small onions, parboiled, and then
    cooked gently in butter
3–4 stuffed olives, sliced
croûtes (see page 93)

Heat the oven to 220°C (425°F) mark 7. Rub salt into the skin of the duckling and prick all over especially around the legs and back. Place in a roasting tin and roast for 45 minutes.

While the duck is cooking, prepare the sauce. Melt the butter in a saucepan and lightly brown the giblets. Add the vegetables and bacon and cook for 5–7 minutes to soften the vegetables. Add the flour and cook gently until golden brown. Add the water, herbs and seasoning. Cover and simmer for 30 minutes. Add the wine, and allow to reduce in volume by one-third, removing any scum as it rises.

Remove the duck from the roasting tin, and cut it into joints. Place the joints in a shallow ovenproof dish, and strain the sauce over. Cover the dish and cook in the oven at 180°C (350°F) mark 4 for 30 minutes, or until the duck is tender.

Garnish with the onions, stuffed olives and croûtes, and serve with new potatoes and peas.

Salmis is the term given to a rich brown stew of duck (or game). It is usual for the duck to be roasted for about three-quarters of the cooking time. It is then finished in a rich brown sauce made from the giblets, with red or white wine added.

ROAST DUCK WITH APRICOTS

Serves 6–8

2 plump ducks, each 1.8–2 kg
  (4–4½ lb)
salt
giblets
1 small carrot, diced
1 small onion, diced
small bunch of herbs
seasoning
575 ml (1 pint) water
1 large can apricot halves
juice of 1 lemon
1 tbsp cornflour
2 tbsp redcurrant jelly
2 tbsp apricot brandy

Heat the oven to 200°C (400°F) mark 6.
Prepare and roast the ducks (see page 39).
Place the giblets in a pan with the carrot,
onion, herbs, seasoning and water. Bring to
the boil, cover and simmer gently for about
1 hour. Strain.

Drain the juice from the apricot halves,
and make the juice up to 575 ml (1 pint)
with the strained giblet stock and lemon
juice. Blend the cornflour with a little cold
water in a basin, add a little of the juice and
mix well. Pour into a saucepan, and bring to
the boil, stirring continuously. Add the
redcurrant jelly and stir to dissolve; add the
apricot brandy. Check the seasoning.

Approximately 10 minutes before the
ducks are cooked, place the apricot halves
in the roasting tin to heat.

To serve, place the ducks, jointed, on a
serving dish, arrange the apricot halves
around, and glaze the ducks with a little of
the sauce. Serve the rest of the sauce
separately.

CASSEROLED DUCK WITH PORT

Serves 4

1 duck
1 medium onion, whole
5–6 sage leaves
seasoning
duck giblets
2 medium onions, chopped
bunch of fresh herbs or bouquet garni
1 tbsp each diced carrot and diced
   celery
425 ml (¾ pint) water or water and
   wine
1 tbsp plain flour
150 ml (¼ pint) port
lemon slices and croûtons (see
   page 93) to garnish

Heat the oven to 150°C (300°F) mark 2.
Place the whole onion and the sage leaves in
the cavity of the duck and season well. Place
the giblets in a saucepan with the chopped
onions, herbs, carrot, celery and seasoning
with the water. Bring to the boil, cover and
simmer for ¾–1 hour. Strain. Place the
duck in a casserole and pour the giblet stock
around. Cover, bring to the boil and cook in
the oven for 1½–2 hours or until the meat is
tender.

Joint the duck, place on a serving dish,
and keep warm. Remove the excess fat from
the cooking juices. Mix the flour with a little
cold water, add a few tablespoonfuls
cooking juices, mix well, and pour into the
casserole with the port. Bring to the boil;
adjust the seasoning as necessary. Pour the
sauce over the duck and garnish with lemon
slices and fried bread croûtons.

This recipe is suitable for an older duck.

ROAST GOOSE

Serves 8

4.5-kg (10-lb) goose
double recipe quantity sage and
   onion stuffing (see page 85)
salt
25 g (1 oz) butter or dripping
watercress to garnish
apple sauce (see page 88)

Heat the oven to 220°C (425°F) mark 7.
Prepare the stuffing. Prepare the goose as
for chicken (see page 8), but cut the wings
off at the first joint before trussing. Place
the stuffing in the cavity from the tail end.
Prick the skin of the goose all over to allow
the excess fat to run out during cooking.
Sprinkle the breast with salt.

Melt the fat in a roasting tin, place the
goose in the tin, and put it in the oven.
Cook for 30 minutes. Reduce the oven
temperature to 180°C (350°F) mark 4;
continue cooking, basting regularly with the

fat which comes from the goose. Allow 35 minutes per kg (15 minutes per lb), but if the goose is old, and perhaps a little tough, allow 45 minutes per kg (20 minutes per lb) and reduce the oven temperature to 170°C (325°F) mark 3.

When the goose is cooked, place it on a serving dish and keep warm. Pour off most of the fat from the roasting dish, and use the residue to make gravy.

Garnish the goose with watercress and serve gravy and apple sauce separately.

To carve, cut off the legs. Remove the wings by slicing a piece of breast meat with each wing. Cut the breast in slices parallel to the breast bone.

Variations
(1) Prune and apple stuffing (see page 86).
(2) Potato stuffing (see page 85).
(3) For garnish, serve fried apple rings or fried pineapple rings.
(4) The gravy is improved if a sour apple is cooked in the roasting tin with the goose.

Using up leftover goose
(1) Slice and eat cold with jacket potatoes, Waldorf salad, or a green salad, accompanied by a damson or quince cheese.
(2) Curried: mince the leftover meat and mix with any stuffing left, plus 1 teaspoonful curry powder, 2 teaspoonfuls plain flour and sufficient gravy to moisten. Season to taste. Place in a greased shallow dish and cook in the oven at 200°C (400°F) mark 6 for 20–25 minutes. Serve with croûtes (see page 93) and any green vegetable.

GAME BIRDS

Game birds, once food for kings, are now
available to all from specialist shops and are a
tasty alternative to poultry for that special
occasion dinner. In this chapter recipes for
different varieties of game bird are given, from
pheasant to the tiny snipe.

ROAST PHEASANT

See page 6 for servings

1 pheasant, trussed (see pages 9–10)
50 g (2 oz) butter
1 medium onion or ½ apple or
  ½ small lemon
salt and pepper
3–4 rashers streaky bacon
150 ml (¼ pint) red wine (optional)
bread sauce (see page 89)
game chips (see page 93)

Heat the oven to 220°C (425°F) mark 7. Place 25 g (1 oz) of the butter in the cavity of the bird, together with the onion, apple or lemon. Rub the remaining butter over the surface of the bird, and sprinkle with salt and pepper. Cover the breast with the bacon. Place the bird in a roasting tin and put in the oven. Cook for ¾–1¼ hours, depending on size, basting regularly. The red wine may be poured into the roasting tin half-way through cooking and although most of it may disappear during cooking, it will give flavour when stock is added to the pan for making gravy.

The giblets should be placed in a pan with water, seasoning and small onion or carrot and cooked gently. The resulting stock should be used with the pan juices from the roasting tin to make a thin gravy.

Garnish the pheasant with watercress, with two tail feathers placed vertically between the legs. Serve with bread sauce, game chips and a green vegetable. Carve as for chicken (see page 15).

GIPSY PHEASANT

Serves 3–4

25 g (1 oz) butter
1 clove garlic, crushed
1 pheasant, jointed (see page 10)
350-g (12-oz) piece of bacon, cubed
2 large onions, sliced
4 ripe tomatoes, peeled and sliced
150 ml (¼ pint) sherry
salt and pepper
¼-½ tsp cayenne pepper

Melt the butter in a flameproof casserole. Add the garlic. Fry the pheasant joints and the bacon until lightly browned. Transfer to a plate. Place the onions in the casserole, and fry gently until soft. Add the tomatoes and cook for 2–3 minutes. Replace the pheasant joints, and pour the sherry over. Season lightly. Cover tightly and simmer gently for about 1 hour, or until the meat is tender. Just before serving, add the cayenne pepper to the sauce.

PHEASANT IN RED WINE

Serves 3–4

1 tbsp oil
50 g (2 oz) butter
1 large pheasant, jointed (see
  page 10)
2 shallots, finely chopped
275 ml (½ pint) red wine
12 button mushrooms
salt and pepper
1 tbsp plain flour

Glazed onions
12 small onions
25 g (1 oz) butter
1 tbsp granulated sugar
150–275 ml (¼–½ pint) stock (see
  page 91)

Heat the oven to 170°C (325°F) mark 3. Heat the oil and 25 g (1 oz) of the butter in a flameproof casserole, add the pheasant joints and sauté gently until golden brown. Remove the joints to a plate. Add the shallots to the casserole and cook gently until soft. Pour in the red wine and combine with the pan juices. Replace the joints in the casserole and add the mushrooms and seasoning. Cover, and cook in the oven for approximately ¾–1 hour, or until the meat is tender. Meanwhile knead together the remaining butter with the flour. When the bird is tender, use the kneaded flour to thicken the sauce as required. Remove any fat from the surface.

While the bird is cooking, prepare the onions. Place them in a pan with the butter and sugar and sufficient stock to barely cover. Cook gently in an open pan until the onions are tender and the stock is reduced to a glaze. Garnish the pheasant with the glazed onions. Serve with creamed potatoes or rice.

NORMANDY PHEASANT

Serves 2–3

1 tbsp cooking oil
25 g (1 oz) butter
1 pheasant
1 small onion, finely chopped
2 tbsp calvados or brandy
150 ml (¼ pint) game or chicken
  stock (see page 91)
2 medium dessert apples, peeled,
  cored and sliced
salt and pepper
150 ml (¼ pint) double cream

Garnish
2 dessert apples, cored and sliced
  into rings
icing sugar
1 tbsp cooking oil
25 g (1 oz) butter

Heat the oil and butter in a flameproof casserole. Gently brown the pheasant, then remove it to a plate. Add the onion to the casserole and fry until softened. Drain off surplus fat. Replace the pheasant in the casserole.

Pour the calvados or brandy into a heated ladle, set alight and pour over the pheasant.

Allow the flame to die, then add the stock and the apples. Cover the casserole tightly, and simmer gently for approximately 45 minutes, or until the pheasant is tender. Remove the pheasant, carve as for chicken (see page 15) and arrange on a serving dish. Keep warm.

Strain the sauce, stir in the cream, reheat, check the seasoning and pour over the pheasant.

Garnish with apple rings that have been liberally sprinkled with icing sugar and fried in the oil and butter.

PEPPERED PHEASANT WITH ALMONDS

Serves 2–3

1 pheasant
50 g (2 oz) butter
1 tsp freshly ground black pepper
1 small onion, chopped
75–100 g (3–4 oz) piece of fat
  bacon
50 g (2 oz) flaked almonds

Heat the oven to 170°C (325°F) mark 3. Mix together the butter and black pepper, and spread over the bird. Place the onion and bacon inside the bird.

Place the bird on a piece of foil, and cover the breast with the almond flakes. Seal the foil, place the bird in a roasting tin and cook for 1½–2 hours. 15 minutes before the end of cooking time, open the foil to allow the breast and almonds to brown.

Serve with an orange and watercress salad.

PHEASANT IN MADEIRA

Serves 4

25 g (1 oz) butter
1 pheasant
4 slices fat bacon, cut small
2 slices ham, cut small
1 medium onion, finely chopped
1 stick celery, finely chopped
1 carrot, finely diced
1 tsp chopped fresh parsley
salt and pepper
pinch of nutmeg
150 ml (¼ pint) Madeira
150 ml (¼ pint) game or chicken
*   stock (see page 91)*
croûtes (see page 93) to garnish

Melt the butter in a flameproof casserole and fry the pheasant, bacon and ham until lightly browned. Transfer to a plate. Fry the onion, celery and carrot until soft. Replace the meats in the casserole. Add the parsley and seasonings. Pour in the Madeira and stock. Cover tightly and cook gently for approximately 1 hour or until the meat is tender.

Place the bird on a serving dish. Liquidize or sieve the sauce, adjust the seasoning and pour over the bird. Garnish with croûtes.

PHEASANT CASSEROLE WITH ORANGE

Serves 3–4

1 tbsp cooking oil
25 g (1 oz) butter
1 pheasant, jointed (see page 10)
225 g (8 oz) mushrooms, sliced
2 tbsp plain flour
275 ml (½ pint) game or chicken
*   stock (see page 91)*
150 ml (¼ pint) orange juice
150 ml (¼ pint) dry white wine
salt and pepper
1 orange

Heat the oven to 180°C (350°F) mark 4. Heat the oil and butter in a frying pan, and add the pheasant joints; fry until browned all over. Transfer the joints to a flameproof casserole. Add the mushrooms to the frying pan and fry for 4–5 minutes, then transfer to the casserole. Sprinkle the flour into the remaining fat, and cook for 2–3 minutes. Mix together the stock, orange juice and wine, and gradually add to the fat and flour. Bring to the boil, stirring all the time, season to taste, and pour into the casserole. Cover tightly, and cook in the oven for approximately 1 hour, or until tender.

Meanwhile peel the zest from the orange and cut into fine strips. Place these in a pan with a little water and simmer gently until soft. Strain. Remove the rest of the peel from the orange and divide it into segments.

When the pheasant is cooked, adjust the

seasoning. Sprinkle the orange strips over the top of the joints, and garnish with the orange segments.

This dish is suitable for an older bird.

ROAST GUINEA-FOWL

Serves 4–5

1 guinea-fowl
4–6 streaky bacon rashers
1 tbsp plain flour
seasoning
275 ml (½ pint) stock using the
  giblets (see page 91)
150 ml (¼ pint) sour cream or
  yoghurt

Stuffing
6–8 olives, stoned and chopped
4 tbsp fresh breadcrumbs
freshly ground black pepper
25 g (1 oz) melted butter
beaten egg

Heat the oven to 190°C (375°F) mark 5. Make the stuffing by mixing the ingredients together, and adding sufficient beaten egg to bind. Place the stuffing in the cavity of the bird. Cover the breast with the bacon rashers and roast for approximately 1 hour, or until the meat is tender, basting frequently.

When cooked, place the bird on a serving dish and keep warm. Sprinkle the flour in the roasting tin and stir into the pan juices. Cook for 2–3 minutes. Gradually stir in the stock, bring to the boil, simmer for 3–4 minutes and add seasoning to taste. Stir in the cream or yoghurt, reheat carefully, and strain into a sauce-boat.

Garnish the guinea-fowl with watercress and serve with game chips (see page 93) and a green vegetable. Carve as for chicken (see page 15).

ROAST PARTRIDGE

Allow 1 partridge for 1–2 persons

For each bird
a knob of butter
seasoning
1 tsp lemon juice
1 rasher streaky bacon
1 vine leaf (optional)

Garnish
croûtes (see page 93)
lemon wedges
watercress

Heat the oven to 220°C (425°F) mark 7. Clean and truss the bird, and place the butter, seasoning and lemon juice in the cavity of the bird. If available, tie a vine leaf next to the skin of the bird with a rasher of bacon over it. Place in a well-buttered tin and roast in the oven for 20–25 minutes. (Alternatively, it may be spit-roasted.)

Serve on a croûte with the pan juices poured over, garnished with lemon wedges and watercress.

As accompaniments, serve fried breadcrumbs, or bread sauce (see page 89), clear gravy and game chips (see page 93).

To carve, cut in half.

COLD PARTRIDGE IN VINE LEAVES

Serves 4

4 young partridges, dressed and
*   trussed (see page 8)*
salt and pepper
4 rashers streaky bacon
8–12 vine leaves (fresh or tinned) or
*   cabbage leaves*

Season the partridges with salt and pepper. Wrap a rasher of bacon around each. Rinse any brine off the vine leaves, and simmer in a little water for 5 minutes. Wrap each bird tightly in 2–3 vine leaves and tie securely. (Cabbage leaves may be used if vine leaves are not available – these need blanching in boiling water, then refreshing in cold water.)

Place the wrapped partridges in a pan, cover with water, bring to the boil, then simmer for 35 minutes.

Plunge immediately into ice-cold water and leave to cool for approximately 10 minutes. Remove the vine leaves and bacon. Serve with a plain green salad, or apple sauce (see page 88), game chips (see page 93) and watercress.

PARTRIDGE WITH CABBAGE

Serves 3–4

1 hard green cabbage, about 900 g
 (2 lb)
salt and pepper
175 g (6 oz) streaky bacon in one
 piece
25 g (1 oz) butter
2–3 partridges (according to size)
8 small onions
2 medium carrots, sliced
225 g (8 oz) pork sausages
bunch of fresh herbs, including
 parsley, thyme and a bay leaf
275–575 ml (½–1 pint) stock (see
 page 91)
2 tsp arrowroot, mixed with 2 tbsp
 cold water

Heat the oven to 170°C (325°F) mark 3. Cut the cabbage into quarters, and cook it in a pan of boiling salted water for 6 minutes. Drain, and refresh in cold water. Divide each quarter into 2–3 pieces. Season lightly.

Place the bacon in cold water, bring to the boil, drain and refresh. Melt the butter in a flameproof casserole and gently brown the partridges, then remove them to a plate. Place half the cabbage in the casserole, and place on top of it the bacon, onions, carrots, sausages and the partridges, with the bunch of fresh herbs. Add some seasoning. Cover with the remaining cabbage, and moisten with stock. Cover tightly, using foil under the lid.

Place in the oven, and cook for 1½–2 hours. If the partridges are young, take them out after 35 minutes; also remove the sausage. Keep covered, whilst the cabbage continues cooking. Check occasionally to make sure it does not become too dry.

Replace the sausages (and partridges if removed) approximately 10 minutes before the end of cooking time to ensure that they are hot.

To serve, cut each partridge in half, the bacon into strips and the sausages into slices. Drain the cabbage, having removed the herbs, and thicken the strained juice with a little slaked arrowroot.

Place the cabbage in a serving dish, arrange the partridges on top, and decorate with the bacon, sausage and onions. Spoon a little of the sauce around the cabbage and serve the rest separately.

This *perdrix aux choux* is a famous French recipe for cooking older birds.

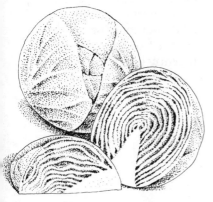

PARTRIDGE WITH MUSHROOMS

Serves 4–6

4 partridges, dressed (see page 8)
50 g (2 oz) butter
225 g (8 oz) mushrooms, sliced
salt and pepper
1 tbsp oil
1 small onion, finely chopped
1 tbsp plain flour
150 ml (¼ pint) dry sherry
425 ml (¾ pint) stock (see page 91)
100 g (4 oz) button mushrooms
chopped fresh parsley to garnish

Melt 25 g (1 oz) butter in a saucepan and cook the sliced mushrooms slowly. Add seasoning. Divide the mushrooms into 4 and stuff the partridge cavities. Melt the oil and the remaining butter in a flameproof casserole and gently brown the partridge. Add the chopped onion and cook for a further 3–4 minutes. Sprinkle in the flour; cook for 2 minutes. Gradually add the sherry and stock and bring to the boil. Season to taste.

Cover and simmer gently for ¾–1 hour, or until the meat is tender. 15 minutes before the end of cooking time, add the button mushrooms. Serve garnished with chopped parsley.

PARTRIDGES IN CREAM

Serves 4–6

4 young partridges
salt and pepper
juice of 2 lemons
25 g (1 oz) butter
1 small onion, chopped
4 slices streaky bacon, chopped
½ tsp dried sage
275 ml (½ pint) single cream

Heat the oven to 170°C (325°F) mark 3. Season the birds inside and outside, and sprinkle with the lemon juice. Melt the butter in a flameproof casserole. Add the partridges and brown all over. Add the bacon and onion and cook for 5 minutes. Add the herbs and the lemon juice and sufficient water to prevent burning.

Cover with a lid, and cook for 30 minutes. Remove from the oven, stir in the cream, heat gently but do not allow to boil. Serve with game chips (see page 93).

PARTRIDGE CASSEROLE

Serves 4

1 tbsp oil
25 g (1 oz) butter
2 partridges, cut in half
4 shallots, chopped
2 carrots, finely diced
small wedge of turnip, finely diced
2 rashers streaky bacon, chopped
150 ml (¼ pint) red wine
275 ml (½ pint) stock (see page 91)
seasoning
beurre manié (see page 92)

Heat the oven to 150°C (300°F) mark 2. Heat the oil and butter in a flameproof casserole and lightly brown the partridges. Transfer to a plate. Gently fry the shallots, carrot and turnip with the bacon. Return the partridges to the casserole, and add the red wine and stock.

Cover and cook in the oven for ¾–1 hour or until the birds are tender. Thicken the sauce with a little beurre manié. Serve with creamed potatoes and pickled red cabbage.

POT-ROASTED PARTRIDGES IN MILK

Serves 4–6

1 tbsp oil
4 partridges (reserve the livers)
2 large onions, quartered
8 small tomatoes
150 ml (¼ pint) sherry
275 ml (½ pint) water
275 ml (½ pint) milk
salt and pepper
2 tbsp capers
2 tbsp parsley
2 tbsp stoned olives

Heat the oven to 150°C (300°F) mark 2. Heat the oil in a flameproof casserole and carefully brown the birds. Add the onions and the whole tomatoes. Cook gently for a further 5 minutes. Pour in the sherry, water and milk. Season with salt and pepper. Bring to the boil and simmer gently. Pound the livers with the capers, parsley and olives in a mortar, and add to the casserole. Cover tightly with foil under the lid, and cook in the oven for approximately 2 hours, or until the birds are tender.

Serve straight from the casserole, accompanied by plain boiled potatoes and Brussels sprouts.

This recipe is suitable for older birds.

ROAST GROUSE

Serves 4

50 g (2 oz) butter
juice of ½ lemon
salt and black pepper
2 young grouse
2 rashers streaky bacon
4 croûtes (see page 93)
1 tbsp oil

Heat the oven to 220°C (425°F) mark 7. Combine the butter and lemon juice and season well with salt and black pepper. Place the mixture inside the birds, and cover the breast of each with streaky bacon.
Stand the birds on the croûtes and place on a roasting tin in the oven. Roast for 25–30 minutes, basting occasionally with oil. Serve on the croûtes, garnished with watercress and slices of lemon.
To carve, cut into joints.

CASSEROLED GROUSE

Serves 4

2 grouse
2 rashers streaky bacon
25 g (1 oz) butter
1 tbsp oil
4 shallots, chopped
2 carrots, chopped
2 tbsp brandy
1 bouquet garni
275 ml (½ pint) red wine
275 ml (½ pint) game stock (see
    page 91)
salt and black pepper
beurre manié (see page 92)
chopped fresh parsley to garnish
lemon slices to garnish

Heat the oven to 150°C (300°F) mark 2. Tie a rasher of bacon around each bird. Heat the oil and butter in a flameproof casserole and lightly brown the birds. Transfer to a plate. Fry the shallots and carrots until soft. Return the birds to the casserole. Heat the brandy and ignite it; whilst it is flaming, pour over the birds. Add the bouquet garni, wine and stock. Season well. Cover and cook slowly for 1½–2 hours, until the birds are tender.
Thicken the sauce with beurre manié. Adjust the seasoning. Garnish with chopped parsley and lemon slices.

ROAST WILD DUCK

Serves 2–4

2 wild duck (any variety)
piece of apple, onion or orange
butter
salt and black pepper
a little red wine, port or orange juice
watercress to garnish

Heat the oven to 220°C (425°F) mark 7. Place a piece of apple, onion or orange in the cavity of each bird, with a knob of butter and seasoning. Season the outside of the bird and smear the breasts with softened butter. Place in a roasting tin and cook for 30–50 minutes for mallard, 30–40 minutes for wigeon, 20–30 minutes for teal. Baste frequently with butter and red wine, port or orange juice. Wild duck is usually served underdone, although this is a matter of taste.

Place on a warmed serving dish and garnish with watercress. Serve with a thin gravy made from the pan juices, having removed the excess fat, or with orange sauce (see page 38). Depending on size, either cut in half or into joints.

POT-ROASTED WILD DUCK

Serves 4

2 wild duck (any variety)
salt and pepper
50 g (2 oz) butter
2 shallots, chopped
1 clove garlic, crushed
1 bouquet garni
1 wine-glass port
juice of 1 orange

Garnish
8 small dessert apples, peeled and
  cored
50 g (2 oz) butter
3–4 tbsp redcurrant jelly
2 tbsp wine vinegar

Heat the oven to 180°C (350°F) mark 4. Season the ducks. Melt the butter in a flameproof casserole and brown the birds. Add the shallots, garlic and bouquet garni. Cover tightly and place in the oven. Cook for 50–60 minutes, basting occasionally.

Meanwhile bake the apples in the oven with the butter until golden brown. Melt the redcurrant jelly in the vinegar and coat the apples.

When the ducks are tender, cut in half and arrange on a serving dish. Keep warm. Skim the fat from the casserole, add the port and orange juice to the juices in the casserole. Bring to the boil and adjust the seasoning. Pour a little sauce over the ducks to glaze, and serve the rest separately.

TEAL WITH ANCHOVIES

Serves 4

4 teal
butter
salt and pepper
75 g (3 oz) cheese, finely grated
8 anchovy fillets
150 ml (¼ pint) stock
   (see page 91)
lemon slices to garnish

Sauce
1 tsp mustard
1 tsp Worcestershire sauce
1 tsp anchovy essence
1 tbsp brown sugar
1 tsp mushroom ketchup
1 tbsp stock (see page 91)
2 tbsp port

Heat the oven to 220°C (425°F) mark 7. Season the teal well, and smear with the butter. Place in a roasting tin in the oven for 20 minutes. Cut each teal in half and place in a casserole. Sprinkle with cheese and place an anchovy fillet on each piece. Moisten with stock, cover and cook at 170°C (325°F) mark 3 for 45 minutes. Meanwhile mix together the rest of the ingredients in a bowl.

When the birds are cooked, transfer them to a serving plate. Pour the sauce ingredients into the casserole and mix with the liquid. Bring to the boil and pour over the birds. Garnish with lemon slices.

PLAIN ROAST WOODCOCK OR SNIPE

See page 7 for servings

1 woodcock or snipe
butter
salt and pepper
fat bacon (one piece per bird)
pieces of bread (one piece per bird)
lemon juice
watercress to garnish

Press the legs and wings together, draw the head around and run the beak through the point where the legs and wings cross. Brush the bird with melted butter, season well and tie a piece of fat bacon around each bird. Spit or oven roast at 220°C (425°F) mark 7. Toast pieces of bread on one side only, and place one under each bird, untoasted side upwards, to catch the juices as they run out from the bird.

Woodcock require cooking for 25–30 minutes, whereas the snipe, being a very small bird, should, as the saying goes, 'fly through the kitchen' and be cooked for 12–15 minutes.

Serve with clear gravy flavoured with lemon juice, and game chips (see page 93).

WOODCOCK WITH ORANGE

Serves 4

4 woodcock
melted butter
salt and pepper
4 rashers fat bacon
4 croûtes (see page 93)
150 ml (¼ pint) white wine
3–4 tbsp concentrated game stock
   (see page 91)
rind and juice of 1 orange
1 tsp melted butter
orange segments to garnish

Prepare and cook the birds as in the previous recipe. Arrange on the croûtes, on a serving dish. Keep warm.

Add the wine and game stock to the pan juices and simmer for 5 minutes. Add the rind and juice of the orange and stir in the melted butter and seasoning. Pour the sauce over the woodcock and garnish with orange segments.

SNIPE WITH MADEIRA

Serves 4

8 snipe, cooked as in recipe opposite
croûtes (see page 93)

Sauce
15 g (½ oz) butter
50 g (2 oz) bacon, finely chopped
3 shallots, finely chopped
2 tsp plain flour
1 tsp tomato purée
50 g (2 oz) mushrooms, chopped
275 ml (½ pint) stock (see page 91)
small bunch of fresh herbs
salt and pepper
75 ml (2 fl oz) Madeira

Cook the snipe as in the recipe opposite. While it is cooking, make the sauce. Melt the butter in a pan, add the bacon and shallot and fry until golden. Stir in the flour, and cook over a low heat until it turns a golden brown colour – stir during this time otherwise the flour will burn. Add the tomato purée, mushrooms and stock. Carefully bring to the boil, stirring; add the seasoning and herbs. Cover and simmer for 15–20 minutes. Strain, add the Madeira and simmer for another 3 minutes.

Serve the snipe on croûtes with a little sauce poured over each, and the remainder of the sauce served separately.

ROAST QUAIL

1 quail per person for a starter, 2
per person for a main course

quail
fat bacon, one rasher per bird
butter
watercress to garnish

Brush the birds with melted butter, and
wrap a rasher of fat bacon around each.
Place in a shallow casserole with butter and
cook at 220°C (425°F) mark 7 for
20 minutes, basting frequently. Serve with
a thin gravy made from the pan juices, and
garnish with watercress.

If available, vine leaves, wrapped around
the birds, will improve the flavour.

QUAIL IN WHITE WINE WITH OLIVES

Serves 4

8 quail
salt and pepper
25 g (1 oz) butter
2–3 rashers streaky bacon, chopped
1 small onion, finely chopped
1 carrot, finely diced
2 tbsp brandy
425 ml (15 fl oz) stock (see page 91)
275 ml (½ pint) white wine
½ tsp dried sage
12 green olives, pitted

Season the quail with salt and pepper. Heat
the butter in a pan and brown the quail.
Transfer them to a place. Add the bacon,
onion and carrot to the pan and fry gently
until the vegetables begin to soften. Replace
the quail in the pan.

Warm the brandy, ignite it and while it is
still flaming, pour it over the birds. Add the
stock, wine, sage and some seasoning, bring
to the boil and simmer gently for
15 minutes. Add the olives and simmer for
a further 10 minutes.

Remove the quail to a serving dish,
return the pan to the heat and boil to reduce
the liquid by half. Pour over the quail.

Serve with plain boiled rice and a
green salad.

QUAIL WITH MUSHROOMS

Serves 2

4 quail
seasoned plain flour
25 g (1 oz) butter
1 tbsp oil
3 rashers streaky bacon, chopped
1 shallot, finely chopped
2 tbsp brandy
100 g (4 oz) mushrooms, sliced
425 ml (15 fl oz) stock (see page 91)
1 bouquet garni or bunch of fresh
  mixed herbs
salt and black pepper
juice of 1 orange
beurre manié (see page 92)

Cut the quail in half and toss in seasoned flour. Heat the oil and butter in a pan and gently brown the quail; transfer them to a plate. Place the bacon and shallot in the pan and fry for 5 minutes.

Return the quail to the pan. Warm the brandy, ignite it and, while it is flaming, pour it over the quail.

Add the mushrooms, stock, herbs and seasoning. Bring to the boil, cover tightly and simmer for 20–25 minutes, until the birds are tender. Add the orange juice.

If necessary thicken the sauce with a little beurre manié. Serve with duchesse or creamed potatoes and glazed carrots.

QUAIL WITH HERBS

Serves 4

8 quail
100 g (4 oz) butter
1 tbsp chopped fresh parsley
1 tbsp chopped fresh summer savory
1 tsp chopped fresh mint
½ tsp chopped fresh thyme
salt and black pepper
8 rashers streaky bacon
150 ml (¼ pint) white wine
150 ml (¼ pint) chicken stock (see
  page 91)
1 tbsp plain flour
croûtes (see page 93)

Heat the oven to 180°C (350°F) mark 4. Place a knob of butter in each quail. Place the birds in a roasting tin, and brush with melted butter. Mix together the herbs and seasoning and sprinkle over the quail. Cover each bird with a rasher of bacon. Mix together the wine and stock and pour it around the birds. Cook in the oven for about 45 minutes, basting occasionally. Remove the bacon rashers. Raise the oven temperature to 200°C (400°F) mark 6, and continue to cook the quail until they are browned and tender.

Place the quail on a serving dish and keep warm. Strain any surplus fat from the roasting tin. Stir the flour into the pan juices. Cook on top of the stove, stirring continuously, until it thickens. Boil for 1 minute. Pour the sauce over the quail and serve with croûtes.

RAISED PIGEON PIE

Serves 6–8

breasts from 2 pigeons
1 tbsp oil
2 medium carrots, diced
1 onion, diced
1 stick celery, sliced
1 bouquet garni
seasoning
275 ml (½ pint) stock (see page 91)
350 g (12 oz) pork sausagemeat
225 g (8 oz) veal or fillet steak cut
* up finely*
2 pickled walnuts, chopped
beaten egg
jelly (made from 275 ml/½ pint
* stock, heated with 1 heaped tsp*
* powdered gelatine)*

Hot water crust pastry
225 g (8 oz) plain flour
75 g (3 oz) lard
¼ tsp salt
scant 150 ml (¼ pint) boiling water

Remove the breasts from the pigeons. Heat the oil in a flameproof casserole and sauté the prepared vegetables until soft. Place the pigeon breasts on top of the vegetables and add stock to come to the top of the vegetables. Add the bouquet garni and seasoning. Braise the breasts until tender. Allow to cool. Heat the oven to 220°C (425°F) mark 7. Grease a raised pie mould, or prepare a collar of doubled greaseproof paper 10 cm (4 inches) deep and 15 cm (6 inches) in diameter. Grease well. Place on a greased baking sheet.

Make the hot water crust pastry by sieving together the flour and salt. Rub in the lard and add most of the boiling water to make a soft dough, mixing well with a knife. Knead gently until smooth. Line the mould or collar with three-quarters of the pastry.

With three-quarters of the sausagemeat, line the inside of the pastry. Mix the veal (or steak) with the walnuts and season well. Place half the mixture in the base of the mould, and lay the pigeon breasts on top. Cover with the remaining veal or steak mixture, and moisten with 3–4 tablespoonfuls stock. Cover with the remaining sausagemeat.

Roll out the last piece of pastry and cover the pie, sealing the edges well. Decorate with pastry leaves as desired. Bake at 220°C (425°F) mark 7 for 15 minutes. Reduce the heat to 170°C (325°F) mark 3 and cook for a further 1¼ hours. Approximately 20 minutes before the end of cooking time, carefully remove the mould or collar and brush the pastry with beaten egg. After removing the pie from the oven, fill with hot, well-seasoned jelly.

PAPRIKA PIGEON

Serves 2–3

2 pigeons
1 tbsp plain flour
2 tsp paprika
salt
50 g (2 oz) dripping
1 onion, sliced
1 clove garlic, crushed
275 ml (½ pint) stock (see page 91)
150 ml (¼ pint) wine
bunch of fresh herbs (parsley, thyme,
   bayleaf) or 1 bouquet garni
2–3 tbsp soured cream or yoghurt
chopped fresh parsley to garnsh

Heat the oven to 170°C (325°F) mark 3. Cut the pigeons in half and toss in the flour mixed with the paprika and salt. Heat the dripping in a flameproof casserole, and fry the pigeons until golden brown. Transfer them to a plate.

Add the onion and garlic to the pan and fry for 5 minutes. Gradually stir in the stock and wine, add the herbs and replace the pigeons in the casserole. Bring to the boil, cover and cook in the oven for 1½–2 hours or until the pigeons are tender. Just before serving, stir in the soured cream or yoghurt. Adjust the seasoning. Sprinkle with chopped parsley.

PIGEON CASSEROLE WITH STEAK

Serves 4

2 pigeons
25 g (1 oz) butter
1 tbsp oil
225 g (8 oz) chuck steak, cubed
2 rashers streaky bacon, diced
275 ml (½ pint) stock (see page 91)
100 g (4 oz) mushrooms, sliced
salt and pepper
1 tbsp redcurrant jelly
1 tbsp lemon juice
1 tbsp plain flour, slaked with
   1 tbsp water
chopped fresh parsley to garnish

Cut the pigeons in half. Heat the butter and oil in a pan and fry the pigeons, steak and bacon until lightly browned. Add the stock, mushrooms and seasoning. Cover tightly and simmer slowly for approximately 2 hours or until the pigeons are tender.

Stir in the redcurrant jelly and lemon juice. Thicken the sauce with the slaked flour. Bring to the boil, cook for 2 minutes, and adjust the seasoning. Sprinkle with chopped parsley to serve.

BRAISED PIGEON WITH ORANGE

Serves 4

4 pigeons
4 small oranges
4 rashers streaky bacon
50 g (2 oz) dripping or butter
4 shallots, chopped
1 tbsp plain flour
150 ml (¼ pint) port or red wine
275 ml (½ pint) stock (see page 91)
salt and pepper
bunch of fresh herbs (parsley, thyme,
  bayleaf, etc.) or 1 bouquet garni
½ tsp crushed coriander
beurre manié (see page 92)
1–2 tbsp Cointreau or Grand
  Marnier (optional)

Heat the oven to 170°C (325°F) mark 3. Remove some thin slices of zest from half the oranges with a potato peeler or zester and place on one side. Place an orange in the cavity of each bird, and wrap a rasher of bacon around each. Secure with string. Heat the dripping in a flameproof casserole, and fry the birds until golden brown. Transfer to a plate. Fry the shallots until golden brown. Stir in the flour and cook for 3 minutes. Gradually stir in the wine and stock and bring to the boil. Add the seasoning. Return the pigeons to the casserole and add the herbs and coriander. Cover tightly and cook in the oven for 1½–2 hours or until the pigeons are tender.

Meanwhile cut the orange zest into strips, place in a small pan with a little water and simmer gently for 15–20 minutes. Strain and reserve the strips.

When the pigeons are cooked, transfer them to a serving dish. Strain the sauce into a saucepan and thicken as necessary with a little beurre manié. Adjust the seasoning and add the orange liqueur. Pour a little over the pigeons and serve the rest separately. Sprinkle the orange strips over the pigeons. Serve with creamed potatoes and broccoli.

CIDER-BRAISED PIGEON

Serves 4–6
1 tbsp oil
25 g (1 oz) butter
4 pigeons
4 rashers bacon

Heat the oven to 180°C (350°F) mark 4. Heat the oil and butter in a flameproof casserole and fry the pigeons. Transfer to a plate. Cut the bacon into 1-cm (½-inch) strips. Add the bacon, onion and carrots, and fry until the vegetables begin to soften.

225 g (8 oz) small onions
2 carrots, sliced
1 tbsp plain flour
275 ml (½ pint) stock (see page 91)
150 ml (¼ pint) dry cider
salt and pepper
225 g (8 oz) mushrooms, sliced

Garnish
2 eating apples
icing sugar
50 g (2 oz) butter
watercress

Stir the flour into the pan and cook for 2–3 minutes; gradually add the stock and cider, stirring until the mixture boils. Season well. Return the pigeons to the casserole, and cover and cook in the oven for 45 minutes.

Add the sliced mushrooms and continue cooking for a further 45 minutes or until the pigeons are tender. Place the pigeons on a serving dish, drain the vegetables and place around the pigeons. Keep hot. Adjust the seasoning of the sauce, and if necessary thicken with a little more flour. Pour the sauce over the pigeons.

During the latter stage of cooking, prepare the garnish. Core the apples, slice into 5-mm (¼-inch) slices. Dust thickly with icing sugar. Melt the butter in a frying pan, and gently fry the apple slices. Garnish the pigeons with apple slices and watercress.

GAME SOUP

Serves 4

1–2 carcases of game, plus giblets if available
1 medium onion, chopped
1 medium carrot, chopped
1 stick celery, sliced
bunch of fresh mixed herbs
6 peppercorns
salt
glass of red wine (optional)
1 litre (1¾ pints) water
beurre manié (see page 92)
2 tsp lemon juice
2 tsp redcurrant jelly

Place the carcases and giblets in a pan with the prepared vegetables, herbs and seasonings. Add the wine and sufficient water to cover. Cover the pan, bring to the boil and simmer for approximately 1½ hours.

Remove the carcase, giblets and herbs. Sieve or liquidize the remaining contents of the pan. Thicken with beurre manié; add the lemon juice and redcurrant jelly. Add any meat from the carcase, finely shredded. Simmer gently for 5 minutes. Serve.

GAME ANIMALS

The meat of wild rabbit, hare and venison has less fat on it than that of domesticated animals and can be dry. This chapter shows how to make many delicious dishes which make the most of the succulent juices and distinctive flavour of these game animals.

ROAST RABBIT

Serves 3–4

1 young rabbit, paunched and
    skinned (see page 11)
6–8 rashers streaky bacon
100 g (4 oz) dripping
25 g (1 oz) plain flour
275 ml (½ pint) stock (see page 91)
bacon rolls (see page 94)

Stuffing
4 heaped tbsp fresh breadcrumbs
50 g (2 oz) shredded suet
salt and pepper
1 tbsp chopped fresh parsley and
    fresh mixed herbs
a little grated lemon rind
a little grated nutmeg
2 tbsp milk

Heat the oven to 200°C (400°F) mark 6.
Make the stuffing: mix the dry ingredients
together and bind with the milk. Place the
stuffing in the rabbit and sew it up. Tie the
streaky bacon rashers over the back. Heat
the dripping in a roasting tin and place the
rabbit in it; covered with greased,
greaseproof paper or foil. Roast for 1 hour,
basting regularly with the fat.

When cooked, remove the paper or foil,
and sprinkle with flour; return to the oven
for about 10 minutes to brown. Transfer to
a serving dish, remove the trussing strings
and keep warm.

Drain most of the fat from the roasting
tin, leaving about 1 tablespoonful. Sprinkle
in the remaining flour, and cook for a few
minutes. Gradually stir in the stock,
ensuring that all the pan juices have been
incorporated. Boil for 4–5 minutes then
strain into a sauce-boat.

Garnish the rabbit with bacon rolls, and
serve, accompanied by redcurrant or quince
jelly, with roast potatoes and green beans.
To carve, cut into joints.

RABBIT IN BEER

Serves 4–5

1 rabbit, about 900 g (2 lb), jointed
  (see page 12)
1 tbsp seasoned plain flour
25 g (1 oz) dripping
100 g (4 oz) streaky bacon, chopped
1 medium onion, sliced
275 ml (½ pint) pale ale
275 mlk (½ pint) stock (see
  page 91)
1 tsp sugar
1 tbsp vinegar
1 bayleaf
1–2 tsp French mustard
12 soaked prunes

Toss the rabbit joints in the seasoned flour. Heat the fat in a heavy saucepan or flameproof casserole, and fry the joints until golden brown. Remove them from the pan.

Add the bacon and onion to the pan and fry until the onion is soft. Pour off any excess fat. Replace the joints in the pan.

Add the ale, stock, sugar, vinegar, bayleaf and mustard. Bring to the boil, cover tightly and simmer gently until almost cooked (1–1½ hours).

Season to taste, add the prunes, and cook for a further 20 minutes. Serve with jacket potatoes and green beans.

RABBIT TENERIFE-STYLE

Serves 4

1 medium-sized rabbit, jointed (see
  page 12)
salt

Marinade
275 ml (½ pint) dry white wine
100 ml (3 fl oz) vinegar
2 sprigs fresh thyme
2 tsp fresh oregano
1 bay leaf

Salmerejo sauce
4 tbsp oil
white wine
2 large cloves garlic
2 tsp paprika
small piece of hot red chilli pepper,
  or ½ tsp cayenne pepper

Place the rabbit joints in a dish and sprinkle with salt. Mix together the ingredients for the marinade and pour over the joints. Allow to stand for a few hours, preferably overnight. Remove the joints and dry thoroughly, reserving the marinade.

Heat the oil in a pan, and gently cook the joints until golden brown all over. Pour the marinade over, adding more wine if necessary to cover the joints. Partially cover the pan and simmer gently.

Meanwhile crush the garlic in a mortar with the paprika, chilli (finely chopped) or cayenne, and a little salt. Add this to the pan and check the seasoning – it should be slightly hot but not over-hot. Continue the cooking for approximately 1 hour or until the meat is tender, adding more wine if necessary. Check the seasoning again before serving.

This tasty dish is one found in any local restaurant in Tenerife. It is a well-flavoured, spicy dish which improves if it is cooked the day before it is required, and then reheated. It is sometimes served with fried potatoes, but more often with fresh crusty bread, and of course, red wine.

RABBIT HOT-POT

Serves 4–6

1 rabbit, jointed (see page 12)
50 g (2 oz) dripping
350 g (12 oz) onions, sliced
225 g (8 oz) carrots, sliced
25 g (1 oz) plain flour
850 ml (1½ pints) stock (see page 91)
450 g (1 lb) potatoes, thickly sliced
bunch of fresh herbs
salt and pepper
melted butter
chopped fresh parsley to garnish
bacon rolls (see page 94)

Heat the oven to 170°C (325°F) mark 3. Place the rabbit joints in cold salted water and leave for 30 minutes to remove the blood. Remove and dry well.

Heat the dripping in a frying pan, and fry the joints until golden brown, then transfer to a casserole. Fry the onions and carrots gently until beginning to soften, and then place on top of the rabbit in the casserole. Add the flour to the remaining fat in the frying pan, and cook for 2–3 minutes. Gradually stir in the stock and bring to the boil.

Place the sliced potatoes in the casserole, season well, pour the sauce from the frying pan over, and add the herbs. Cover tightly and cook in the oven for approximately 2 hours or until the rabbit is tender.

30 minutes before serving, the lid may be removed and the potatoes brushed with melted butter. Return the casserole to the oven without the lid, to brown the potatoes. Check the seasoning. Serve garnished with chopped parsley and bacon rolls.

CASSEROLED RABBIT

Serves 4–5

1 rabbit, jointed (see page 12)
175 g (6 oz) streaky bacon, cut into
  strips
350 g (12 oz) onions, finely chopped
1 tbsp chopped fresh parsley
salt and pepper
stock (see page 91)
1 tbsp plain flour
forcemeat balls (see page 87
  variation)

Heat the oven to 150°C (300°F) mark 2. Layer the bacon, rabbit and onions in a deep casserole, sprinkling the parsley and seasoning between the layers. Add sufficient stock to just cover. Cover with a tightly fitting lid and cook in the oven for approximately 2 hours or until the meat is tender.

Mix the flour with a little water in a basin, add several tablespoonfuls gravy from the casserole. Pour it all into the casserole and bring to the boil.

Adjust the seasoning and serve with forcemeat balls and redcurrant jelly, accompanied by jacket potatoes and carrots.

TASTY RABBIT

Serves 4–5

1 rabbit, jointed (see page 12)
salt and pepper
1 small onion, finely chopped
2 tsp dried or fresh mixed herbs
2 bay leaves
4 cloves
575 ml (1 pint) water and vinegar
  mixed
25 g (1 oz) butter
1 tbsp oil
225 g (½ lb) onions, finely chopped
plain flour

Place the rabbit joints in a deep dish and sprinkle with salt and pepper and add the onion, and the herbs. Cover with the water and vinegar mixture, and leave to soak overnight. Remove from the liquid, and dry the joints thoroughly. Reserve the liquid.

Heat the butter and oil in a strong saucepan or a flameproof casserole, lightly brown the rabbit joints, add the remaining onions and gently fry. Pour over the marinade in which the rabbit was soaked. Cover tightly and simmer gently for 1½ hours. Just before serving, thicken the gravy with a little flour, and adjust the seasoning. If the flavour is a little sharp, a teaspoonful sugar will rectify this.

This is good served with jacket potatoes and a green vegetable.

RABBIT & SAUSAGE CRUMBLE

Serves 4–5

1 rabbit, jointed (see page 12)
375 g (12 oz) sausagemeat
225 g (8 oz) onions, chopped
1 tbsp chopped fresh herbs
stock (see page 91)
75–100 g (3–4 oz) fresh
    breadcrumbs
salt and pepper
25 g (1 oz) butter

Heat the oven to 150°C (300°F) mark 2. Place half the sausagemeat in a casserole and lay the rabbit joints on top. Sprinkle with the chopped onion and herbs, and some salt and pepper. Place the remaining sausagemeat on top. Half-fill the dish with stock.

Cover with the breadcrumbs, pressing down well, and put small knobs of butter on top. Cover with foil, and cook for 1½ hours or until the rabbit is tender. 15 minutes before the end of cooking, remove the foil to allow the top to brown.

Serve with creamed potatoes and a green vegetable.

CURRIED RABBIT

Serves 4

1 rabbit, jointed (see page 12)
25 g (1 oz) butter
1 tsp oil
2 large onions, chopped
1 large apple, chopped
½–1 tbsp curry powder
1½ tbsp plain flour
575 ml (1 pint) stock (see page 91)
1 tbsp sultanas
1 tsp chutney
1 tsp redcurrant or gooseberry jelly
seasoning

Heat the oven to 170°C (325°F) mark 3. Heat the butter and oil in a frying pan and fry the rabbit joints until golden brown, then transfer them to a casserole. Add the chopped onion to the pan and fry until soft, then sprinkle over the rabbit, together with the chopped apple.

Put the curry powder and flour in the frying pan and fry for 1–2 minutes. Add the stock gradually, and bring to the boil. Add the remaining ingredients and pour into the casserole. Cover tightly and cook for 1½–2 hours, or until the meat is tender. Adjust the seasoning and, if too sweet, a little lemon juice will rectify this.

Serve with boiled long grain rice.

ROAST HARE

Serves 4–6

1 leveret
6 rashers fat bacon
100 g (4 oz) dripping
1 tbsp plain flour
575 ml (1 pint) strong stock (see
  page 91)
1 wine-glass port
1 tbsp redcurrant jelly
salt and pepper
watercress and lemon slices to
  garnish

Stuffing
175 g (6 oz) fresh breadcrumbs
1 medium onion, finely chopped
50 g (2 oz) shredded suet
the liver, parboiled and finely
  chopped
1 tbsp chopped fresh parsley
½ tbsp chopped fresh thyme, or
  marjoram
grated rind and juice of 1 lemon
grated nutmeg
salt and pepper
1 egg

Heat the oven to 200°C (400°F) mark 6. Prepare the hare (see pages 11–12). Mix the stuffing ingredients together and add sufficient beaten egg to bind. Place in the cavity of the hare. Sew up and truss. Tie the rashers of bacon around the hare.

Place the hare in a roasting tin with the dripping. Cover and place in the oven. Roast for 1½–2 hours, basting regularly. When the hare is nearly cooked, remove the bacon rashers and sprinkle with the flour. Return to the oven, uncovered, and cook for a further 20 minutes, basting occasionally, until well browned. Transfer the hare to a hot serving dish, and remove the trussing strings.

Strain off any fat from the roasting tin, add the stock, port and jelly, and simmer for about 5 minutes. Adjust the seasoning. If the sauce is too sweet, a little lemon juice may be added. Strain the sauce into a sauce-boat.

Garnish the hare with watercress and lemon slices. Serve with roast potatoes, fresh green vegetables and redcurrant jelly. To carve, cut into joints.

To roast hare of doubtful age
Prepare and truss the hare so that it will fit into a steamer. Steam until tender, leaving unstuffed. Place the hare in a roasting tin and cook as in the recipe above. Serve with forcemeat balls (see page 87) which may be roasted with the hare for the last 15 minutes.

JUGGED HARE

Serves 8

1 hare, paunched, skinned and cut
    into neat pieces (see pages 11–12)
2 tbsp bacon fat
2 large onions, each stuck with
    1 clove
4–5 peppercorns
1 stick celery, sliced
1 carrot, quartered
1 tsp whole allspice
bouquet garni of fresh herbs
juice of 1 lemon and a strip of rind
salt
½–1 litre (1–2 pints) stock (see
    page 91)
beurre manié (see page 92)
1 large glass port or glass of the
    marinade
blood of the hare
2 tsp redcurrant jelly

Marinade
150 ml (¼ pint) red wine
1 tbsp oil
1 shallot, sliced
2 bay leaves
freshly ground black pepper
6 juniper berries, crushed
salt

Prepare the marinade: place all the ingredients in a pan, bring to the boil, remove from the heat and allow to cool. Place the hare in a deep dish, and pour over the cold marinade. Leave to stand several hours, or preferably overnight.

Remove the hare pieces from the marinade and dry well. Heat the oven to 140°C (275°F) mark 1. Heat the bacon fat in a frying pan and quickly brown the hare pieces. Pack into a deep casserole with the vegetables, spices, bouquet garni, lemon rind, juice and salt. Barely cover with stock. Either cover tightly with foil before closing the lid of the casserole, or seal the edges of the lid with a flour and water paste. Place the casserole in a deep pan of hot water and cook in the oven for 3 hours.

Remove the lid, pour off the gravy into a pan, and remove the vegetables and bouquet garni. Thicken the gravy with sufficient beurre manié to produce a thin creamy consistency, bring to the boil and remove from the heat.

Add several spoonfuls of gravy to the hare's blood then carefully pour it back into the pan; add the port (or strained marinade) and redcurrant jelly. Adjust the seasoning. When the jelly has melted, pour the gravy over the hare and reheat gently.

Serve hot with forcemeat balls (see page 87 main recipe), accompanied by braised red cabbage.

This is a classic dish which was originally cooked slowly in a deep earthenware 'jug', standing in a deep pan of hot water, in a slow oven.

HARE IN BEER

Serves 5–6

1 small hare, jointed (see page 12)
blood of the hare
1 tbsp plain flour
1 tsp paprika
50 g (2 oz) dripping
1 clove garlic, crushed with salt
2 medium onions, each stuck with
    2 cloves
575 ml (1 pint) brown ale
1 wine-glass port
salt

Heat the oven to 150°C (300°F) mark 2. Toss the hare joints in the flour mixed with paprika. Heat the dripping in a flameproof casserole and fry the joints until evenly brown. Add the crushed garlic, onions and brown ale. Bring to the boil, cover tightly and place in the oven. Cook slowly for 3–4 hours or until the meat comes off the bone. Remove the onions. Add several spoonfuls of the gravy to the blood in a basin, mix well and pour back into the casserole. Add the port, and heat gently without boiling. Adjust the seasoning.

Serve with reducurrant jelly, boiled potatoes and broccoli.

SADDLE OF HARE WITH CREAM

Serves 4

1 good plump hare, paunched and
    skinned (see page 11)
French mustard
25 g (1 oz) butter
150 ml (¼ pint) strong stock (see
    page 91)
150 ml (¼ pint) cream

Marinade
3 tbsp oil
2 small onions, sliced
2 small carrots, sliced
275 ml (½ pint) red wine vinegar
150 ml (¼ pint) red wine
large sprig fresh thyme
2 bay leaves
small sprig fresh rosemary
6 peppercorns
salt

To prepare the marinade, heat the oil in a pan, add the vegetables and cook gently until soft. Add the remaining marinade ingredients, bring to the boil and simmer for 7 minutes. Pour into a large bowl and leave to cool.

Joint the hare (see page 12), leaving the back (saddle) whole. Place all the hare in the marinade and leave for 36 hours, basting and turning occasionally. Remove the saddle – the rest of the hare should be put on one side and dealt with separately. Spread the saddle with mustard.

Heat the oven to 170°C (325°F) mark 3. Melt the butter in a flameproof casserole, and gently brown the saddle. Strain the marinade and pour over the saddle, then simmer until the marinade is reduced by about one third. Pour on the stock – the saddle should be barely covered. Bring to the boil, cover tightly and cook in the oven until absolutely tender (about 1¾ hours).

Remove the saddle to a serving dish. Add the cream to the remaining contents of the casserole and boil up well for a few minutes. Adjust the seasoning. Strain the sauce, pour a little over the hare, and serve the rest separately in a sauce-boat. Serve with game straws (see page 93) and green beans.

HARE & GROUSE PIE

Serves 4–6

1 casserole grouse
225 g (8 oz) stewing beef
2–3 joints of hare (fore-legs)
1 lamb's kidney, halved and sliced
50 g (2 oz) mushrooms, chopped
1 small onion, finely chopped
100 g (4 oz) streaky bacon, diced
stock (see page 91)
salt and pepper
225 g (8 oz) flaky pastry
forcemeat balls (see page 87
    variation)

Heat the oven to 220°C (425°F) mark 7. Make the forcemeat balls (see page 87).

Divide the grouse into 4 portions, cut the beef into strips, and cut the hare joints into smaller pieces. Layer the meats, mushroom, onion and bacon in a 1½-litre (2½-pint) pie-dish. Season well between the layers. Barely cover with stock. Place the forcemeat balls on top.

Roll out the pastry and cover the dish, decorate the edges, and make 4–6 pastry leaves with the trimmings for the top. Brush with beaten egg. Bake in the oven for 15 minutes. Reduce the heat to 170°C (325°F) mark 3, and bake for a further 1½ hours or until the meat feels tender. If the pastry browns too quickly, cover the pie with a piece of greased greaseproof paper. Serve hot or cold.

ROAST HAUNCH OF VENISON

Serves 6–8

1 haunch of venison
olive oil
100 g (4 oz) butter
350 g (12 oz) fat bacon rashers
plain flour and water paste to cover
    the joint
1 tbsp plain flour

Marinade
275 ml (½ pint) red wine
275 ml (½ pint) water
1 clove garlic, crushed
1 tbsp onion, chopped
1 tbsp carrot, chopped
1 stick celery, chopped
50 g (2 oz) mushrooms, sliced
6 peppercorns
bay leaf

Sauce
1 tbsp plain flour
seasoning
juice of ½ orange

Make the marinade by placing all the
ingredients in a saucepan, bring slowly to the
boil, boil for 2 minutes and allow to cool.
Place the venison haunch in a deep dish and
pour the cold marinade over. Marinate for
1–3 days, basting and turning the joint 2–3
times a day. When ready, remove the joint
from the marinade and dry well. Reserve the
marinade.

Heat the oven to 230°C (450°F) mark 8.
Rub the joint with olive oil, and cover with
pats of butter. Wrap the bacon around the
joint. Cover with the flour and water paste,
or wrap in cooking foil. Place the joint in a
roasting tin, and put in the oven for 15
minutes. Reduce the temperature to 150°C
(300°F) mark 2 and roast the joint, allowing
55 minutes per kg (25 minutes per lb) for red
deer, and 35 minutes per kg (15 minutes per
lb) for roe or fallow deer.

15 minutes before the end of cooking time,
crack the paste open, or unwrap the foil.
Remove the bacon rashers, sprinkle the joint
with flour, and baste well. Raise the oven
temperature to 200°C (400°F) mark 6 and
return the haunch to the oven for 15 minutes
to brown.

Place the haunch on a serving dish. Pour
the cooking juices out of the paste case or foil
into a pan and skim off some of the fat.

Mix the flour with salt and pepper and a
little of the strained reserved marinade. Add
to the pan juices, with more marinade as
required, and the orange juice. Stirring,
bring to boil, and simmer for 3–4 minutes.
Adjust the seasoning and serve in a sauce-
boat.

Serve the venison accompanied with
redcurrant jelly, roast potatoes and a purée of
celeriac. Carve as for a leg of lamb.

ROAST SADDLE OF VENISON

Serves 6–8

1 saddle of venison, 2–2.5 kg
  (4–6 lb)
8–12 rashers streaky bacon
150 ml (¼ pint) port (optional)
beurre manié (see page 92)

Marinade
425 ml (¾ pint) red wine
150 ml (¼ pint) red wine vinegar
275 ml (½ pint) water
4 tbsp oil
2 sprigs fresh thyme
6 juniper berries, crushed
2 bay leaves
1 blade of mace
piece of orange rind (zest only),
  about 2.5 cm (1 inch) square

Trim the saddle, removing any hard skin. Place the saddle in a deep dish. Mix together the ingredients for the marinade, and pour it over the saddle. Allow to marinate for about 2 days, turning and basting 2–3 times daily.

Heat the oven to 200°C (400°F) mark 6. Remove the saddle from the marinade and dry well. Strain and reserve the marinade.

Place the bacon rashers over the top of the saddle and tie in place. Put the saddle in a roasting tin and cover tightly with foil. Place in the oven. After 30 minutes, reduce the temperature to 180°C (350°F) mark 4 and continue cooking (55 minutes per kg/25 minutes per lb for red deer, and 35 minutes per kg/15 minutes per lb for fallow deer). During the cooking period, baste the saddle every 15 minutes with the marinade.

15 minutes before the end of cooking time, remove the foil, and remove the bacon rashers, reserving them for garnish. Sprinkle the port over the saddle and raise the oven temperature to 200°C (400°F) mark 6 and allow the saddle to brown.

Transfer the saddle to a serving dish. Add more marinade or water to the juices in the roasting tin, to make up to about 575 ml (1 pint). Stir over the heat to blend and thicken with beurre manié. Strain the sauce and serve separately.

To carve, slice the meat across the ribs, parallel to the backbone, carving from the narrow end of the joint to the wide end (i.e. tail to head).

Serve the saddle with redcurrant jelly, game chips (see page 93) and a purée of celery or chestnuts.

VENISON STEAKS WITH RED WINE SAUCE

Serves 4

4 slices (1–2 cm/½–¾ inches thick)
  from the loin or haunch
salt and freshly ground pepper
25 g (1 oz) butter
1 tbsp oil
4 juniper berries, crushed
1 good sprig fresh rosemary
150 ml (¼ pint) soured cream or
  yoghurt
salt and pepper
lemon slices to garnish

Marinade
2 shallots, finely chopped
strip of lemon rind
pinch of celery salt
200 ml (7 fl oz) red wine

Lay the venison slices in a dish and season well with salt and freshly ground pepper. Add the ingredients for the marinade, and pour the wine over. Cover and leave to marinate for up to 2 days. Remove the meat from the marinade and dry thoroughly. Reserve the marinade.

Heat the oil and butter in a large frying pan and gently brown the steaks on each side. Add the juniper berries and rosemary, and cover the pan. Lower the heat and cook gently until the meat is tender (for about 30–40 minutes).

Remove the steaks from the pan, place on a serving dish and keep warm. Strain the marinade into the pan, and dissolve the pan juices. Boil up to reduce the liquid a little. Add the soured cream (or yoghurt) and simmer for 2–3 minutes. Check the seasoning. Pour the sauce over the meat and garnish with lemon slices.

Serve with potatoes (sautéed in butter) and a tossed green salad.

VENISON STEAKS WITH CHERRIES

Serves 5–6

700 g (1½ lb) loin of venison
  (without bone) or slices from the
  top of the haunch
3 tbsp oil
120 ml (4 fl oz) red wine or port
freshly ground black pepper
225 g (8 oz) canned cherries, stoned

Slice the venison into 2-cm (¾-inch) steaks, and place them in a shallow dish. Sprinkle over 1 tablespoonful oil and the port or wine, with a liberal grinding of pepper. Cover and leave for a minimum of 1 hour.

To make the sauce, heat the oil in a saucepan, add the vegetables and venison trimmings and cook gently until the vegetables start to soften and brown lightly. Add the flour and continue to cook gently until the flour becomes a golden brown colour. Gradually stir in two-thirds of the

Sauce
75 g (3 oz) onion, diced
75 g (3 oz) carrot, diced
1 small stick celery, diced
trimmings from the venison
2 tbsp oil
1 tbsp plain flour
*575 ml (1 pint) game stock (see
    page 91)*
25 g (1 oz) mushrooms, chopped
½ tsp tomato paste
small bunch of fresh herbs
120 ml (4 fl oz) red wine
2 tbsp red wine vinegar
1 tbsp redcurrant jelly

stock, and add the mushrooms, tomato paste, herbs and wine, bring to the boil, partially cover and simmer for 25 minutes. Remove any scum as it rises. Add half the remaining stock and bring to the boil, skimming again. Add the rest of the stock, reboil, and skim. Strain the sauce into a clean pan, add the vinegar and the redcurrant jelly, bring to the boil, and simmer for 5–6 minutes until the jelly is dissolved. Add the cherries.

Meanwhile, remove the venison from the marinade, and dry thoroughly. Heat 2 tablespoonfuls oil in a frying pan, and fry the venison in it for about 4 minutes on each side.

Reboil the sauce. Arrange the venison steaks on a flat serving dish, with cherries at each end, pour a little sauce over the steaks and serve the rest separately.

Serve with game chips (see page 93) and artichoke hearts.

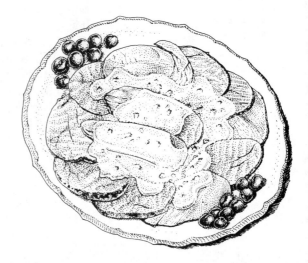

BRAISED VENISON

Serves 5–6

1.5–2 kg (3–4 lb) haunch or loin of
venison

Marinade
4 tbsp oil
100 g (4 oz) carrots, sliced
100 g (4 oz) onions, sliced
50 g (2 oz) celery, sliced
1 clove garlic, sliced
575 ml (1 pint) red wine or wine
and water
6 juniper berries, crushed
sprig of fresh rosemary, sprig of fresh
thyme and 3–4 fresh parsley
stalks, tied together
1 bay leaf

Mirepoix
1 tbsp oil
225 g (8 oz) carrots, diced
225 g (8 oz) onions, diced
100 g (4 oz) celery, sliced
100 g (4 oz) turnip, diced

Stock
beurre manié (see page 92)
1 tsp redcurrant jelly

To make the marinade, heat the oil in a pan,
add the vegetables and cook gently to
soften. Add the remaining ingredients,
bring to the boil and simmer for
30 minutes. Leave until cold.

Place the venison in a deep dish, pour the
marinade over, leave up to 3 days, basting
and turning the venison 2–3 times daily.

Heat the oven to 190°C (375°F) mark 5.
Remove the venison from the marinade,
and dry well. Strain and reserve the
marinade.

Heat the oil for the mirepoix in a pan, add
the vegetables, and gently sauté them until
softened. Place the vegetables in a deep
casserole and moisten them with some of
the marinade. Place the venison joint on top
and add sufficient stock to come a quarter of
the way up the joint. Cover tightly and place
in the oven. Cook for 1½–2 hours or until
the meat is tender. Remove the meat, carve
into slices, and place on a serving dish, and
keep warm.

Strain the gravy from the casserole into a
saucepan. Place it over the heat and reduce
it a little, skimming off any fat. Thicken
with beurre manié and add the redcurrant
jelly. When the jelly is dissolved, check the
seasoning. Pour some of the gravy over the
sliced meat and serve the rest separately.

Serve with potato and celeriac purée and
green beans.

RAISED GAME PIE

Serves 6–8

350 g (12 oz) shoulder or neck
  venison
2 tbsp sherry
450 g (1 lb) hot water crust pastry
  (see page 64)
4 rashers streaky bacon
beaten egg to glaze

Filling
225 g (8 oz) pig's liver, minced
1 medium onion, finely chopped
225 g (8 oz) pork sausagemeat
1 hard-boiled egg
1 tsp chopped fresh parsley
½ tsp chopped fresh thyme
2–3 juniper berries, crushed
seasoning

Prepare a collar of doubled greaseproof paper, 10 cm (4 inches) deep and 18 cm (7 inches) in diameter. Grease well. Place on a greased baking sheet. Cut the venison into fine strips and sprinkle with the sherry. Cover and leave to marinate for at least 1 hour.

Heat the oven to 190°C (375°F) mark 5. Make the hot water crust pastry (see page 64). Use three-quarters of the pastry to line the base and sides of the collar, ensuring there are no thin places. Line with the streaky bacon. Mix the ingredients for the filling together. Place one-third of the filling in the base of the mould and cover with half the venison. Continue filling the mould with alternate layers, finishing with a layer of the filling. Cover the pie with the remaining pastry, ensuring that the edges are well sealed. Use any trimmings to make pastry leaves for decoration. Make a 1-cm (½-inch) hole in the centre of the top. Bake in the oven for approximately 1½–2 hours. If the pastry appears to be browning quickly reduce the temperature after ¾–1 hour to 170°C (325°F) mark 3. 20 minutes before the end of cooking, remove the paper collar and brush the pastry well with beaten egg.

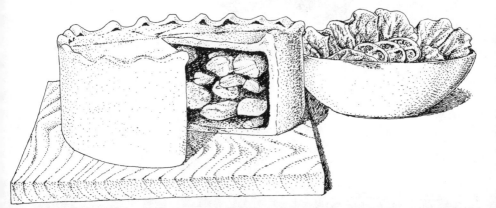

STUFFINGS, SAUCES AND GARNISHES

This chapter shows how to make a variety of
tasty sauces and stuffings for both poultry and
game as well as traditional accompaniments
such as game chips and bacon rolls.

SAGE AND ONION STUFFING

75 g (3 oz) onion, chopped
175 g (6 oz) fresh breadcrumbs
2 tsp fresh chopped sage
3 tbsp melted butter (or margarine)
  or 50 g (2 oz) grated suet
salt and pepper
beaten egg

Place the onion in a pan with a little water and simmer gently until soft. Drain well and mix with the dry ingredients. Add sufficient beaten egg to bind.

Both this stuffing and the parsley and thyme one (page 88) may be shaped into balls, rolled in seasoned flour and baked in the roasting tin around the bird, or in a separate tin for 40–45 minutes, basting and turning occasionally.

SAUSAGE AND CHESTNUT STUFFING

25 g (1 oz) butter
1 tbsp oil
1 turkey liver
100 g (4 oz) streaky bacon, chopped
100 g (4 oz) onion, chopped
225 g (8 oz) chestnuts, peeled and
  chopped
450 g (1 lb) pork sausagemeat
1 tbsp fresh chopped parsley
salt and pepper

This stuffing is suitable for turkey. Heat the oil and butter in a frying pan and fry the turkey liver until firm and the bacon until crisp. Remove from the pan. Chop the liver into small pieces. Fry the onion until soft.

Place all the ingredients in a large bowl and mix well to thoroughly combine. Allow to get cold before using to stuff the neck end of a turkey.

Any remaining stuffing may be formed into balls and cooked as in the recipe for sage and onion stuffing (above).

POTATO STUFFING

225 g (8 oz) onions, finely chopped
550 g (1¼ lb) potatoes
75 g (3 oz) butter or double cream
1 tbsp fresh chopped sage
salt and pepper

This stuffing is good for goose. Place the onion in a pan with sufficient water to cover and simmer gently until soft. Drain well. Boil the potatoes, and drain well. Mash the potatoes and blend in the butter or cream. Stir in the sage and onions, mix well and season to taste.

ANCHOVY AND HERB STUFFING

175 g (6 oz) fresh breadcrumbs
1 rasher streaky bacon, chopped
1 medium onion (or 4 shallots),
    finely chopped
2 tsp chopped chives
1 tsp fresh thyme
2 tsp fresh chopped parsley
4–6 anchovy fillets, chopped
grated rind and juice of ½ lemon
6 tbsp melted butter or 50 g (2 oz)
    shredded suet
beaten egg

This stuffing is good for roast hare. Mix all the dry ingredients together, add the lemon juice and melted butter (if used) and bind with beaten egg.

PRUNE AND APPLE STUFFING

15–20 prunes (depending on size)
575 ml (1 pint) red wine, or water,
    or wine and water mixed
700 g (1½ lb) cooking apples

This stuffing is good for goose. Soak the prunes in the wine or water overnight. Remove the stones. Peel, core and quarter the apples. Use to stuff the cavity of a goose after it has been seasoned.

PORK AND HERB STUFFING

1 medium onion (or 4 shallots),
    finely chopped
25 g (1 oz) butter
450 g (1 lb) shoulder pork, minced
100 g (4 oz) fresh breadcrumbs
1 tbsp fresh chopped parsley
1 tsp fresh thyme and 1 tsp fresh
    marjoram, or 1 tsp mixed dried
    herbs
½ tsp ground nutmeg
beaten egg
salt and pepper

This stuffing is suitable for turkey. Melt the butter in a pan and gently fry the onion until soft. Mix all the ingredients together, season well and bind with the beaten egg.

OATMEAL STUFFING

50 g (2 oz) butter
1 small onion, chopped finely
100 g (4 oz) medium oatmeal
1 tbsp fresh chopped parsley
salt and pepper
milk to mix

This stuffing is suitable for chicken. Heat the butter in a pan and gently fry the onion until soft. Add the oatmeal, parsley and seasoning. Mix well. Add milk to moisten further if necessary, but do not make it too wet. Allow to cool before using.

CELERY STUFFING

4 sticks celery, finely chopped
1 small onion, chopped
25 g (1 oz) butter
1 tbsp oil
175 g (6 oz) fresh breadcrumbs
salt and pepper

Heat the butter and oil in a pan and gently cook the celery and onion for 5 minutes. Add the breadcrumbs and seasoning, mix well, adding a little melted butter, if necessary, to bind.

FORCEMEAT BALLS

1 small onion, finely chopped
1 rasher bacon, chopped
4 tbsp fresh breadcrumbs
1 tbsp suet
1 tbsp fresh chopped parsley
1 tbsp fresh lemon thyme or
    marjoram
beaten egg
breadcrumbs and butter for frying

Cook the onion with the bacon until soft. Add the rest of the ingredients, mix well and bind together with beaten egg. Shape into balls, coat in egg and breadcrumbs and fry in butter until golden brown.

Variation
Omit the onion and bacon, and do not coat in egg and breadcrumbs or fry in butter.

PARSLEY AND THYME STUFFING

100 g (4 oz) fresh breadcrumbs
1 tbsp chopped fresh parsley or 2 tsp dried parsley
2 tsp fresh thyme or 1 tsp dried thyme
½ tsp grated lemon rind
salt and pepper
2 tbsp melted butter (or margarine) or 40 g (1½ oz) grated suet
beaten egg

Mix the ingredients together in a bowl, and add sufficient beaten egg to bind – take care not to add too much otherwise the stuffing will be hard.

APPLE STUFFING

700 g (1½ lb) cooking apples, peeled, cored and diced
50 g (2 oz) butter
salt and pepper
1 tsp grated lemon rind
2 tbsp sugar
225 g (8 oz) fresh breadcrumbs

Prepare the apples and cook gently in the butter until soft. Add the remaining ingredients, and moisten with a little water if necessary.

APPLE SAUCE

450 g (1 lb) cooking apples
25 g (1 oz) butter
2–3 tbsp water
strip of lemon rind
sugar to taste

Peel, core and thickly slice the apples. Place in a pan with the butter, water and lemon rind. Cover and cook gently until soft (a good cooking apple should fluff up during cooking and it should not be necessary to sieve it). Remove the lemon rind, and beat well with a wooden spoon until smooth (or pass through a coarse sieve). Add sugar to taste.

BÉCHAMEL SAUCE

275 ml (½ pint) milk
1 small onion, stuck with 4 cloves
1 piece carrot
sprig of fresh parsley
blade of mace
6 peppercorns
25 g (1 oz) butter
25 g (1 oz) plain flour
salt

Place the milk in a saucepan with the onion, carrot, parsley, mace and peppercorns and bring slowly to the boil. Remove from the heat, cover and allow to infuse for 20–30 minutes, then strain. In a clean pan, melt the butter, add the flour and cook for 2–3 minutes. Gradually add the milk, stirring constantly, bring to the boil, and simmer for 2 minutes. Check the seasoning. Use as required.

CRANBERRY SAUCE

450 g (1 lb) cranberries
100 g (4 oz) sugar
2 tbsp port (optional)

Place the cranberries in a pan, add sufficient water to cover, bring to the boil and simmer gently, bruising the cranberries with a wooden spoon, until reduced to a pulp. Stir in the sugar and port, and cook until the sugar is dissolved.

BREAD SAUCE

275 ml (½ pint) milk
1 small onion, stuck with
   3–4 cloves
blade of mace
1 bay leaf
75–100 g (3–4 oz) fresh
   breadcrumbs
salt and pepper
pinch of ground nutmeg
25 g (1 oz) butter

Place the milk in a saucepan with the onion, mace and bay leaf and bring slowly to the boil. Remove from the heat, cover and leave to infuse for 15–20 minutes. Remove the onion, blade of mace and bay leaf. Stir in the breadcrumbs with the seasoning and butter, and beat well.

ESPAGNOLE SAUCE

1 rasher bacon, chopped
25 g (1 oz) butter
1 tbsp oil
100 g (4 oz) onion, chopped
100 g (4 oz) carrot, chopped
25 g (1 oz) plain flour
575 ml (1 pint) stock (see page 91)
50 g (2 oz) mushrooms, chopped
1 tbsp tomato purée
bunch of fresh mixed herbs or
   bouquet garni
salt and pepper
1 glass sherry

Heat the butter and oil in a pan and fry the bacon, add the onion and carrots and fry gently to soften. Sprinkle in the flour and cook gently to a golden brown colour. Gradually add the stock and bring to the boil, stirring constantly. Add the mushrooms, tomato purée and herbs. Cover and simmer for approximately 30 minutes. Strain into a clean pan, add the sherry and season to taste.

POIVRADE SAUCE

Make as for espagnole sauce (see above) but use marinade and red wine vinegar for part or all of the stock.

The zest and juice of 1 orange may be added together with 1 tablespoonful redcurrant jelly.

DEMI-GLACE SAUCE

Make as for an espagnole sauce (see above), but add half the stock to start with, bring to the boil and simmer for 30 minutes, skimming as necessary. Add half the remaining stock, boil for 5 minutes, skim, add the remaining stock and repeat the process. Strain into a clean pan, add the sherry, and cook to a consistency which will coat the back of a spoon.

GIBLET GRAVY

giblets (heart, liver, gizzard and
     neck)
1 small onion
1 small carrot
small piece of celery
bunch of fresh herbs or bouquet garni
6 peppercorns
salt and pepper
575–850 ml (1–1½ pints) water
cooking juices from the roasting tin
1 tbsp plain flour

Place the giblets in a pan with the onion,
carrot, celery, herbs, peppercorns and salt
and 575 ml (1 pint) of the water in a pan.
Bring to the boil, cover and simmer for at
least 1 hour, or for the duration of the bird's
cooking time.

Strain the stock and make up to 575 ml
(1 pint) with water. Pour a little into the
roasting tin in which the bird was cooked
(excess fat having been removed) and stir
around well to ensure that all the pan juices
have been incorporated. Blend the flour
with a little cold water in a basin, add some
of the stock and pour into a saucepan. Add
the remaining stock. Stir until it boils,
adjust the seasoning and simmer for
2–3 minutes.

This gravy is suitable for any bird.

STOCK

carcase of chicken (or other poultry
     to suit recipe) plus giblets if
     available, or carcase of game
1 medium onion, sliced
2 medium carrots, sliced
1 matchbox-sized piece of swede,
     diced
1 stick of celery, sliced
1 bouquet garni, or bunch of fresh
     herbs
seasoning

Place the ingredients in a saucepan with
sufficient water to cover. Bring to the boil
and remove any scum as it rises. Simmer for
1½–2 hours. Strain into a bowl and use as
required. Should a strong stock be required
for a recipe, the stock should be placed in a
saucepan and boiled to reduce the volume
and concentrate the contents.

Stock may be frozen or stored in a
refrigerator. If not required the day of
making, cool quickly and freeze or store.
Reboil the next day if not required.

MAYONNAISE

1 egg yolk
½ tsp salt
¼ tsp pepper
½ tsp dry mustard
2 tbsp white wine vinegar or
*   distilled malt vinegar*
150 ml (¼ pint) salad oil

Place the egg yolk with the seasonings in a basin, add half the vinegar and mix well with a wooden spoon. Dribble in the oil, a little at a time, beating well. When all the oil has been incorporated, add more vinegar as necessary. Season to taste.

VINAIGRETTE DRESSING

2 tbsp white wine vinegar, or
*   distilled malt vinegar*
½ tsp salt
¼ tsp dry mustard
¼ tsp pepper
4 tbsp salad oil
1 small whole clove garlic,
*   (optional)*

Place all the ingredients in a screw-top jar and shake vigorously to form an emulsion.

Variations
2 shallots, very finely chopped or 2 tablespoonfuls finely chopped fresh parsley or 1–2 teaspoonfuls finely chopped chives may be added to the basic dressing.

BEURRE MANIÉ (KNEADED BUTTER)

butter
plain flour

This is a liaison for thickening sauces.
   Use twice as much butter as flour, and work them together to form a paste. Add small pieces to the contents of a pan or casserole, off the heat. The butter melts and draws the flour into the liquid.

CROÛTES AND CROÛTONS

slices of bread
butter for frying (optional)

Croûtes are thick slices of bread, cut in squares or circles, either fried in butter or toasted. Small game may be served with and/or cooked on croûtes.

Croûtons are small dice or fancy shapes of bread, usually fried, but may be toasted. The fancy shapes are used to garnish savoury dishes. The small dice are used to garnish soup.

GAME CHIPS

potatoes
deep fat/oil for frying
salt

Peel the potatoes, and shape into cylinders. Slice very finely into wafers (the use of a mandolin slicer would be advantageous). Soak in cold water to remove the surface starch. Heat the oil to 190°C (375°F).

Drain the potato wafers, and dry thoroughly. Lower them gently into the hot oil, and keep them moving to prevent them sticking. After 1–2 minutes, the wafers will rise to the surface of the oil, indicating that they are nearly cooked. Watch carefully as they change colour. They should be golden brown and crisp. Drain the wafers and sprinkle with salt.

GAME STRAWS

potatoes
deep fat/oil for frying

Peel the potatoes, and cut into 3-mm (⅛-inch) slices. Cut each slice into 3-mm (⅛-inch) sticks. Soak in cold water to remove the surface starch. Heat the oil to 190°C (375°F).

Drain the straws and dry thoroughly. Lower the straws into the hot oil and keep shaking the basket gently to keep the straws separate. Fry for 3–4 minutes, then remove from the oil. Reheat the fat, and again lower the straws into the oil, and cook for approximately 1 minute until the straws are golden brown and crisp. Drain, and serve immediately.

BACON ROLLS

Allow 1–2 rolls per person

rashers of streaky bacon

Take rashers of streaky bacon, place on a board, hold one end of a rasher with the left hand, and with a firm palette knife, working from left to right, stroke the bacon to stretch it. Cut into 7.5-cm (3-inch) lengths, roll up each length and secure with a skewer. Grill or cook in the oven until crisp.

INDEX